T0012987

Andrea Grace's Gentle Sleep
Solutions for Toddlers

Also available by Andrea Grace

Does your baby have trouble sleeping? You're not alone. Designed specifically for the very many parents encountering the same issues as you, this practical, no-nonsense book gives you the insights, tools and strategies to help your baby get the rest they need – however difficult the challenge.

WHAT PARENTS SAY

'We loved Andrea's method because it was gentle, kind and based around the needs of the baby.'
'Andrea has transformed our lives, she is amazing, a sleep guru!'
'I trusted Andrea and the results spoke for themselves from the very start.'
'I can't recommend Andrea Grace highly enough.'

Andrea Grace's Gentle Sleep Solutions for Toddlers

ANDREA GRACE

First published by Sheldon Press in 2023
An imprint of John Murray Press
A division of Hodder & Stoughton Ltd,
An Hachette UK company

2

Copyright © Andrea Grace 2023

The right of Andrea Grace to be identified as the Author of the Work
has been asserted by her in accordance with the Copyright, Designs and
Patents Act 1988.

All rights reserved. No part of this publication may be reproduced,
stored in a retrieval system, or transmitted, in any form or by any means
without the prior written permission of the publisher, nor be otherwise
circulated in any form of binding or cover other than that in which
it is published and without a similar condition being imposed on the
subsequent purchaser.

This book is for information or educational purposes only and is not
intended to act as a substitute for medical advice or treatment. Any
person with a condition requiring medical attention should consult a
qualified medical practitioner or suitable therapist.

A CIP catalogue record for this title is available from the British Library

Trade Paperback ISBN 978 1 399 80383 0
eBook ISBN 978 1 399 80384 7

Typeset by KnowledgeWorks Global Ltd.

Printed and bound in Great Britain by Clays Ltd, Elcograf S.p.A.

John Murray Press policy is to use papers that are natural, renewable and
recyclable products and made from wood grown in sustainable forests.
The logging and manufacturing processes are expected to conform to the
environmental regulations of the country of origin.

John Murray Press
Carmelite House
50 Victoria Embankment
London EC4Y 0DZ

www.sheldonpress.co.uk

Contents

Meet the author   vi

Introduction   viii

1 Sleep: the facts and background   1
2 What every child needs for a good night's sleep   9
3 Problems with falling asleep   20
4 Night-time sleep problems   42
5 Naps   74
6 Tricky little challenges   82
7 Family life   100
8 Additional needs and common physical sleep issues   120
9 Understanding why your child is struggling with
   sleep, and preparing for change   142
10 Taking control and helping your child to sleep
   well – the techniques   160

Index   193

Meet the author

Welcome to *Andrea Grace's Gentle Sleep Solutions for Toddlers*

Hello! I am Andrea Grace, an experienced baby and child sleep expert, nurse, mental health nurse, health visitor and mother of four.

I am known for my gentle approach to parenting and sleep, which respects the individuality of each child and their family.

I believe that toddlerhood is a glorious, fascinating (and often hilarious) time and that it can sometimes have its tricky moments when it comes to their sleep. Toddlers are easily overwhelmed by their emotions and this is *especially* true when they are tired. Sleep is a massively important part of their life, and as well as helping to keep them on an emotional even keel, it is also very important for their physical and mental health, development and happiness.

It is absolutely essential too that you get the sleep that you need so that you can enjoy the challenging and beautiful job of being a parent.

What I know from my experience is that if you get to the bottom of why a toddler is wakeful and then you put in place an approach that feels right for you and which addresses their particular situation and their individual needs; the end result is a contented, sleeping child and a confident and well-rested parent.

Therefore, I want to reassure you that it is possible to teach your toddler to sleep well in a way that is supportive, encouraging, safe and gentle.

I hope that my Gentle Sleep Solutions for Toddlers helps your child and you get the sleep that you need.

For William, Celia, Theo and Annabel. My beautiful children who have taught me so much.

Introduction

A few years ago I wrote a book about baby sleep, titled *Andrea Grace's Gentle Sleep Solutions*.

Its aim was to help parents understand why their babies struggle with sleeping, and to offer a choice of solutions according to the nature of their own baby and the reason for the sleep problem. The book has, at its heart, a respect for the individuality of the baby and for people's own style of parenting.

Gentle Sleep Solutions is still going strong, and parents like it because it explains some of the science behind sleep and offers choices of approach, rather than a one-size-fits-all sleep plan.

Now I have written *Andrea Grace's Gentle Sleep Solutions for Toddlers* (well, two- to five-year-olds, really) as it is not only little babies who struggle with sleeping. In my work as a sleep specialist, I help just as many families with over-twos as those with babies.

Sometimes, sleep problems in young children are carried on from babyhood, and sometimes they are new – arising from their natural development, growing independence and imagination.

Typical questions that parents ask me are: How can I help my child to feel safe when they are scared of being alone at bedtime? What do I do if they come into my bed every night? How do I know when they ready to drop their nap? How do I help them sleep well if they are ill or have special needs?

These questions are all answered in this book – and there are many more, too, as children's sleep problems are numerous and can sometimes be complex. In the various chapters I will share the knowledge that I have, so that you can understand what might be going on in your child's mind when it comes to sleep struggles, along with the advice that you need to help them.

The solutions I offer are all emotionally safe and can be used according to the type of sleep problem that your child has. *Most* importantly, you can choose a solution which you know will suit the individual nature and temperament of your own child.

As with the original *Gentle Sleep Solutions*, this book doesn't recommend a single approach or formula, but, rather like having a personal consultation with me, offers choice, insight and guidance.

I've been a child sleep specialist for over 25 years and have worked directly with thousands of families to get them the sleep that they need. Even more have been helped by reading my book, articles and social media posts.

Before specializing in childhood sleep, I was (and still am) a registered nurse, a psychiatric nurse and a health visitor. My approach to helping babies and children is a moderate, sensible one which is non-judgemental and based on science, up-to-date research and my own experience.

As well as my professional involvement in child health care, I have four children of my own and each of them were *completely* different as little ones. They all had wobbles with their sleep at one time or another, and what might have worked to help one of them, was not guaranteed to help the other. Between them, they have taught me so much. One of my boys has autism, and he in particular has not only brought me a massive amount of joy but has also helped me to understand what is truly important when it comes to nurturing a growing child – providing a safe and loving environment, with lots of predictable routines, a respect for their individuality and a sense of humour!

This very personal experience with my own family has taught me that you are led by the child that you have. Different toddlers respond to different routines/settling techniques/activities and so on, and there could never be a wholesale parental approach to sleep that is right for every child.

My hope is that, by using this book, you will gain the understanding and skills to help your toddler to sleep well, whatever they are like, and in a way that feels right and suits your parenting style.

1

Sleep: the facts and background

Why we sleep

Sleep is a necessity for life and health, just as food and drink are.

As parents, we give our children the most nutritious and delicious food that we can, and we also need to make sure that they get enough sleep. Good sleep habits and associations learned in young childhood can last a lifetime, and teaching your child how to sleep well when they are little, is one of the best things that you can do for them.

Sleep is critical for so many functions, but when it comes to toddlers these are the especially important ones:

- memory consolidation and learning
- brain development and health
- growth hormone release
- emotional regulation
- concentration, decision making and problem solving
- creativity
- feeling happy and content
- eating well
- enjoying exercise and play
- having fewer accidents
- resistance to infection.

So making sure that your child gets enough sleep will keep them healthier and happier and will even give them a head start with their learning, at school and nursery.

The circadian rhythm

As humans, we are naturally inclined to sleep at night and be wakeful in the day. Although it might not feel like it always, your child is no different. We all have an internal biological 'clock' which works to tell us the difference between night and day. Your little one produces sleep/wake hormones which help them to sleep more at night and eventually begin to nap for shorter periods before stopping sleeping during the day at all, unless they are unwell or on a long journey. This is called the circadian rhythm.

This **circadian clock** (or biological clock) is situated in an area of the brain known as the hypothalamus. In order to work well, the circadian clock needs external clues such as differing levels of light and darkness. It also responds to conditions within your child's own body, such as temperature, hunger and hormone levels.

You can help your child to have a healthy, functioning circadian rhythm by giving them regular bedtimes and wake-up times. Generous exposure to daylight, especially in the morning, will help to set their biological clock to sleep well at night, and so it's good to get outside to the playground or park if you can. Even having breakfast in the brightest room in the house will help. At night, having the room as dark as possible will help them sleep better.

The nature of your child's sleep at night

When your child goes to sleep at bedtime, they don't just pass out for the night and then wake in the morning. They naturally wake up from time to time as they go through the different stages of sleep, and this is absolutely healthy and normal. Your child experiences periods of light sleep and deep sleep at different times in the night. They may shout out, rock around the cot or bed, have different facial expressions and seem to be very busy in their sleep. Much of their behaviour as they sleep is determined by which kind of sleep they are in. There are two main types: **rapid eye movement** (REM) sleep and **non-rapid eye movement** (NREM) sleep. If you can understand these two kinds of sleep, you will be better able to understand what's happening when your child wakes in the night.

NREM sleep (deep sleep)

This is the conventional sleep that we mean when we say that someone is 'fast asleep'. It is broken down into three stages:

- **Stage 1** – during this stage the sleeper becomes drowsy and nods off but can still be woken up. Stage one lasts from a few seconds to about 5 minutes. During this stage your child might jerk or startle, but don't panic – these **hypnic** or **hypnagogic jerks** are normal.
- **Stage 2** – the beginning of falling into a deeper sleep, this stage lasts for about 5–25 minutes. Your child is less likely to be disturbed by external noises but it is still possible.
- **Stage 3** – this is the deepest sleep stage and lasts for about 30–45 minutes. It is also known as 'delta sleep' or 'slow wave sleep' due to the brain wave patterns observed during sleep recordings.

During NREM sleep, your child's eyes will move slowly under their eyelids, and your child is more likely to lie still. Their breathing is slow and regular, and they look peaceful. Growth hormone is released, and muscle growth and repair happens. Your child's immune system becomes busy when they are in deep sleep, producing cytokines which are chemicals that help to protect them against and fight infections.

REM sleep (light sleep)

REM sleep happens when your child is coming out of deep sleep, just over an hour to an hour and a half after they have first fallen asleep, and it lasts for about 5 minutes. This is when the brain becomes very active and dreaming tends to happen. You will see your child's eyes moving rapidly under their eyelids, and although their muscle tone is low at this time, you might see them make little twitching or jerking movements. Their breathing speeds up and their mouths might move. During REM sleep the experiences that your child has had during the day are stored in their 'memory bank'. **This memory consolidation is very important for learning.**

REM sleep is strongly connected to a child's brain development. For an adult, about a quarter of a typical night is spent in REM. Babies spend about half the night in REM and then, as they mature, that time very gradually decreases until they get to about five or six years old, when their REM/NREM proportions are the same as an adult's. After being in REM sleep, it is usual to stir or wake up. This wake-up is biologically normal, and there is no need to assume that your child has woken up because there is something wrong. Don't worry – they are not poorly, hungry or lonely!

Sleep cycles

When a child closes their eyes and goes to sleep for the night, their sleep happens in cycles, made up of some NREM sleep and some REM sleep, followed by an 'arousal' – in other words, a stirring or waking (Figure 1.1). So, as I said, it is *completely* normal for your child to wake up in the night and even 'perfect sleepers' do so, but the difference is that these children go back to sleep without needing any help.

One thing that is really important to know when you're trying to make sense of your child's sleep (or lack of it) is that their

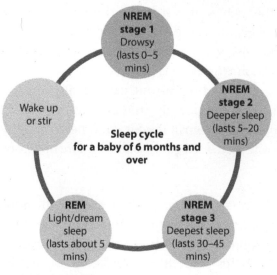

Figure 1.1 Your child's sleep cycles

sleep is naturally deeper at the beginning of the night, and as morning approaches, they become more wakeful because there is less NREM (deep) sleep and more REM (light) sleep within each cycle.

When your child was a baby, up until the age of about six months, their sleep cycle was about 50 minutes, but as a toddler or young child now, it is roughly the same length as an adult's. As we know, though, they experience a bit more REM sleep, and this means that they have a tendency to be more restless in their sleep.

Sleep hormones

Melatonin

Melatonin is sometimes called 'the hormone of darkness', and it helps your child to fall asleep and to stay asleep. After the age of about three months, children naturally make this miracle sleep aid all by themselves. It is stimulated by daylight and produced in the pineal gland. As the evening approaches, melatonin levels naturally increase, getting them ready to fall asleep. To encourage healthy melatonin levels, it is good to have their bedroom as dark as possible, as light at night-time can actually impair melatonin production. This is especially true of blue light (the kind commonly emitted by screens). If your child needs a night light, it is best to use one with a red glow, as this is more melatonin friendly.

Cortisol

Cortisol, which is produced in the cortex of the adrenal gland, is the hormone associated with wakefulness. Later in the night, as morning approaches, levels of this 'awake hormone' begin to rise, and this helps your child to wake up for the day. Cortisol is also a stress hormone and sometimes a child will produce too much of it, causing them to be wakeful (even when they are still tired) when they wake too early in the morning, or to struggle to settle to sleep when they are tired at bedtime. The most common reason for young children having high cortisol levels are:

- being overtired
- bedtime conflict and feeling upset
- too much noise
- too much light exposure – especially to screens.

Melatonin versus cortisol

Under the influence of the circadian clock, these two hormones *should* work in harmony to regulate your child's sleep and wake patterns. If a child is overtired, however, and goes to sleep at night with high levels of cortisol, this can lead to very broken sleep and/or early waking.

We'll look at this later, but you might just find it useful to know that putting your child to bed later because they wake very early in the morning may be counterproductive.

Sleep pressure and awake windows

Hopefully, you can see how sleep is influenced by the circadian rhythm and hormone levels, but there is also another really important factor that affects the way that your child sleeps. This is called homeostasis, and it is the way the body regulates and maintains its health and balance. Things like body temperature and hunger levels are controlled by the body's homeostasis – and so is sleep.

To feel sleepy, we all need to experience a rise in **sleep pressure**. Sleep pressure builds up when we are awake, and we call these periods of wakefulness **awake windows**. The younger the child, the more quickly the build-up of sleep pressure and the smaller the awake windows. As the child gets older, the awake windows naturally space out and eventually they will drop their daytime nap, but the child then naturally needs an earlier bedtime. Typically, a two-year-old will need an awake window of about 5–6 hours before being ready to sleep for the night. When they drop their nap, they will have an awake window of about 12 hours – for example waking at 7 a.m. and going to bed at 7 p.m.

As we know, when children are overtired, they can feel stressed and this causes a rise in cortisol and sometimes adrenaline – both of which fight against the sleep hormones. With this in mind, it is good to keep an eye on their awake windows and give your child the opportunity to sleep when they need to, so that they are not overtired, but also have a long enough awake window to be able to go to sleep when it is bedtime.

How much sleep do toddlers really need?

The average amount of sleep for a two- to three-year-old is 12 hours, and some of this sleep will be taken during the day. For three- to five-year-olds, the average amount of sleep is eleven and a half hours. Most toddlers drop their nap by five years old, although some will continue to sleep in the day occasionally – especially if they are on a car journey. Sometimes, if a child is still napping regularly or *wanting* to nap when they are over five years old, it can be a sign that they are not getting enough night-time sleep.

Children can differ in the amount of sleep that they need. Generally speaking, as they get older, they sleep more soundly at night and need less sleep in the day. That is one of the reasons why most children have outgrown their need for a nap by about five years old. There are times, of course when they need more sleep, such as when they are unwell, having a growth spurt, or coping with starting school or nursery.

It's good to remember that, even though your child might seem wide awake and full of energy, they still need around 10–14 hours sleep a day, and that most will need a bit of help to switch off, get calm and relax into sleep.

Below is a guide to the approximate hours of sleep needed by children of different ages, up until their teens.

Age	Daytime sleep	Total hours of sleep
12–24 months	1–3 hours	11–14 hours
2–3 years	0–3 hours	10–14 hours
3–5 years	0–1.5 hours	10–13 hours
6–12 years	0	9–12 hours
Teens	0 (unless you count the time spent in bed in the morning!)	8–10 hours

2

What every child needs for a good night's sleep

A good bedtime routine

A bedtime routine is simply a repeated series of steps leading up to bedtime, which help a child to prepare mentally and physically for sleep. A really consistent routine can make them feel both sleepy and safe, and having a good bedtime routine is one of the best things you can do to help your child to sleep well.

The best bedtime routines are *very* repetitive, and this is important, as young children like to be able to predict what is coming next. In fact, they thrive and feel safe with familiarity and predictability. When the bedtime routine regularly culminates with them falling asleep, they often become conditioned to feel sleepy towards the end of their familiar bedtime 'script'.

An established and familiar bedtime routine is great for parents, too, as it gives you a well-practised structure to follow at the end of the day. Being a parent of a toddler is very hard work, and as their bedtime approaches, everyone, including you, will be tired. It really helps when you can switch on to 'autopilot' and not have to think too hard about what to do next. Just because a bedtime routine is established and consistent (strict!), it doesn't mean that it can't also be fun and loving. It *should* incorporate cuddles and little songs/rhymes/games along the way, such as in the bath, while cleaning teeth, and so on.

Having a nightly bath or shower is a great way for your child to expend their energy reserves, and you shouldn't worry if it seems to energize them. If they are running around and giddy afterwards, this is *normal*, and they will settle down when they get into bed if you direct them to. This nightly bath or shower serves as a marker that the day is finished and it's now time for bed. Even if your child protests, even if they have dry skin or eczema (and you have to apply emollients afterwards), even if you personally are low on energy and don't really have the will to get the flannel out, it's worth having some kind of washing ritual at the end of the day – not only for hygiene but also because it is so important for their sleep. Depending on your circumstances, your routine can be as long or as short as you like, provided that it is familiar.

Here's an example of the kind of routine that you might want to try. Don't worry if the last bullet point is something that you and your child are finding difficult – later in this book, I'll give you some advice to help you get there.

- Begin your routine about half an hour before you know your child is ready for sleep.
- If they have been watching TV, turn it off now and remove any screen devices.
- The *sequence* of the routine is more important than the *timing*, and it's a mistake to start the routine too early. It needs to culminate in them getting into bed, rather than coming back into the living room for stories or playtime.
- Take everything that you need for the night with you, to avoid having to come back into the living area.
- Follow a similar bedtime 'script' by using familiar phrases and actions at key points during the routine.
- Give your child a bath or shower every night if you can.
- Have a final visit to the toilet if you're doing potty training.
- Go directly to your child's sleep room from the bathroom.
- Clean nappy/pull-up on if they need one, and get them dressed for bed.

- Give a drink of milk if your child is still having it, and if they have the milk in a bottle, don't let them fall asleep as they are drinking it. Keep the bedroom light on or the curtains open, so that the room isn't dark.
- *After* the milk, read stories together, sitting on their bed together or with them on your knee if they are still in a cot. The final story should be the same each night, so that it becomes a sleep trigger.
- Put them into their cot or bed while they are still fully awake.
- Kiss them good night and leave the room.

Loving boundaries

When babies grow into children, they develop their sense of independence and they increasingly make their own choices.

Sometimes, especially during toddlerhood, making decisions about what they want can be overwhelming for them and this is especially true when they are tired. Most parents will be familiar with the following situation: You're trying to placate a tired, upset child by suggesting what it is that they need. 'Do you want this toy? A drink? Are you hungry? Have you got a tummy ache?' Often, a tired child doesn't know what they want; all they know is that they are not feeling good.

Asking questions of anyone (young or old) who is feeling tired or out of sorts can be overwhelming and will only add to any feeling of stress, and for this reason I always advise parents to *give directions* at bedtime rather than asking too many questions. Throughout the bedtime routine it is better for you to be nicely in charge, and so, instead of asking 'Shall we clean your teeth now?' or 'Do you want to put your pyjamas on?' it's more effective to say, 'Come on! Teeth time!' and 'Let's put your pyjamas on!'

Children feel safe when they know that their parents are taking on all the responsibility. When they feel safe, it makes it easier for them to fall asleep – knowing that all is well and they've nothing to worry about.

I'm not suggesting that the only interaction that you have with your child should be you telling them what to do. Most of the time, you will be *encouraging* your child to make choices and express their needs. It's just that, at bedtime, it works really well when you, rather than they, are leading things.

Having a bedtime routine in place, along with you being clear in your own mind that you are the leader, will help you set these loving boundaries.

I gave this advice to a family whose little girl of three was really struggling with bedtimes. When her mum started giving her directions instead of asking her permission, the little girl initially objected and told her mum, 'Go back to work, and get Dad!' Mum, however, did manage to keep her resolve, despite the challenges, and improve the sleep of her funny and sweet daughter.

The right timing

About a quarter of young children have problems falling asleep at bedtime. For some of these children, getting into bed is the signal that now it's time to play, or cry, or keep getting up and coming down. It can be so frustrating for both parent and child when this happens.

From the child's point of view, they are only following their usual routine and doing what they have learned to do. They're not happy to see that Mummy or Daddy is getting cross or tearful, but their habit of continual 'curtain calls' is something that they can't really help either.

From an adult's point of view, it is both maddening and often *worrying* that putting your child to bed is the start of an exhausting rigmarole that lasts sometimes for an hour or more and means that they don't get to sleep until way past their ideal bedtime. Added to this, bedtime settling problems often lead on to night-time waking, so you may well be up in the night with them, too. It's just as well that toddlers are so gorgeous because otherwise this situation would be too much to bear.

Often, these bedtime struggles can be overcome by understanding how important timing is when it comes to scheduling bedtime and what the best bedtime for your child should be.

Towards the end of the day, children begin producing the sleep hormone, melatonin. This is the hormone that helps to put them to sleep and which also *keeps* them asleep. Melatonin production typically starts about 2–3 hours before bedtime. So if your child usually goes to sleep at 7.30 p.m., they will naturally start producing melatonin between 4.30 and 5.30 p.m.

Melatonin isn't the only thing that helps them to fall asleep, however. If you cast your mind back to the previous chapter, you might remember that children also experience a build-up of **homeostatic sleep pressure** when they have been awake for a certain length of time. It is this build-up of sleep pressure (or sleep drive), combined with the melatonin already in their system, that makes them feel sleepy and enables them to drift off.

In a nutshell, for most children between two and five years old, there is a 'golden time', usually between 6 p.m. and 8 p.m. when the build-up of sleep pressure and sleep hormones come together to make them at their most biologically ready to sleep.

However, you and I both know that not every child is the same, and for some children, their melatonin production kicks in later. This can be due to lots of different factors, including having had too much screen time or not enough exposure to daylight earlier on, having a learning difference, or it being simply the way they are made.

Some families actually want to have a late bedtime for their children – to have them up with them in the evenings and then have a later start in the morning. These children will naturally start to have raised melatonin levels close to their usual bedtime.

One thing is for sure, though: putting a child to bed with too much energy to spare can make getting to sleep very difficult for them and can set up an association of bedtime as playtime, or worry time, or procrastination time!

On the other hand, leaving a child to become overtired can cause a rise in both cortisol and adrenaline levels, both of which are stress or 'wakeful' hormones, which will damp down the effects of melatonin.

Establishing a regular and happy bedtime **which culminates in them falling asleep at the end** can condition a child to fall asleep even if they are overtired or not tired enough. Please remember this, because it's important! The power of the routine can often override factors such as insufficient melatonin, too little sleep pressure, and even overtiredness.

Positive sleep associations

Sleep associations can also be called 'sleep cues' or 'sleep triggers'. Simply put, they are things and behaviours which, especially if they are pleasant, will help your child to fall asleep. Many of these sleep associations happen during a child's bedtime routine – for example, the same little rhyme or phrase spoken when they put their pyjamas on. Each repeated element that is part of a bedtime routine, whether it is a ritual of drying between their toes or kissing them good night, will become a lovely sleep association for them, and – as we've already discussed – children love repetition.

Lots of children will develop positive sleep associations around external things and objects – the most obvious ones being their dummy, their thumb, a 'lovey', a special blanket or their teddy, or twiddling their hair, which can help them to relax and go to sleep. These comforters are known as 'transitional objects' and, as the name suggests, can be very useful in helping young children make the transition from awake to asleep and also from dependence to independence! They help little ones feel more secure when separating from you – at the nursery or crèche, for example. Because a comforter helps a child to feel safe, calm and happy, you shouldn't worry about how grubby and worn it is. However, if possible, you should get an identical 'spare' if you can, so that you can rotate them for cleaning, and have a back-up if one gets lost. If your child is very attached to a comfort object, it is a healthy sign that they are growing up and learning how to cope with their independence. At least half of all babies and toddlers have a comforter, and most will choose their own object at around six months old. Interestingly, their need for the comforter tends to be at its greatest between 18 months and two and a half years old.

Other positive sleep associations are environmental, such as low lighting levels, white noise, the familiar smell and feel of their bedding, and even the sound of you chatting in the living room.

It's great if their familiar sleep cues support them to fall asleep without having you in the room or in the bed with them, but for lots of children the one sleep association that they need to fall asleep is *you*! This can be an unhelpful sleep association, as it may not be sustainable. It is a positive association in many ways because it is lovely to stroke your child's face or let them twiddle your hair until they fall asleep, for instance, but it doesn't work in the long term to *keep* them asleep.

Insight

It's really common for babies and toddlers to twiddle their parent's (usually their mum's) hair as they go to sleep. Another thing that some like to do is stroke or pinch their parent's skin or nipple. Although this provides the child with lots of comfort, it can cause Mummy or Daddy a lot of discomfort!

As you know, it is normal and healthy for children to wake up in the night, and if they fall asleep with you next to them, and wake up later and you've gone, they are very likely to feel upset. Naturally, they will need to find you, and then you will have to do the same thing again in the night ... and again ... and again, until you get up in the morning having had hardly any sleep.

If this works for you and you are happy with the situation, then there is no need to change things, but it's a shame for your child to feel upset in the night and feel compelled to call for you when it is equally possible for them to learn how to sleep happily on their own.

The other thing about your child needing you to be their sleep association and lie with them as they go to sleep is that, if it takes a long time and you daren't move until they are asleep, because you're not 'allowed' to, you can feel like you're being held hostage. That feeling of you not being in control is not good for you, and it's not good for your child either.

A safe and pleasant sleep environment

Not every child has their own room, and in fact there are lots of advantages to siblings sharing a room together when they are little. Whether your child has a room of their own, is sharing with a sibling, sleeping in your room with you, or indeed if all the family sleep in the same room, the most important things to consider about your child's sleep space are:

- the bed or cot
- the room temperature
- the lighting
- the ambience.

We'll look at each of these in turn.

The bed or cot

It is perfectly OK for children of three years old, and even beyond that, to sleep in a cot. So, unless you need the cot for a new baby, and provided that your child isn't climbing out of it and risking hurting themselves, then I would suggest that, if you're all sharing, you keep them in the cot for as long as possible. Remaining in the cot maintains familiarity and continuity. It also gives you a little bit more control to pop in and out of the room, without them running after you.

When it comes to moving them out of the cot, there are so many beautiful beds available – but the princess bed, racing car bed or mini four-poster is not going to be the key to helping your child sleep well. You should choose a bed that feels right to you, fits nicely into your child's space and is the right size for them.

A younger child may need safety guards fitting to the sides of the bed to prevent them rolling out. For that reason, children's beds tend to be lower to the ground than standard single beds. If your child is in a toddler bed converted from their cot bed, they will be at a safe height.

Just as when they were a baby, your child needs to sleep on a firm, flat surface and the mattress needs to fit securely into the bed frame with no gaps at the side. Many children simply have a mattress on the floor or a futon, and this is fine. Sleeping on cushions or a bean bag is not good for them, as they need a very flat surface to support their growing spine and young, soft bones.

Once they are over two years old, your child can have a pillow if you want to give them one, but it is not necessary, until they need it for sitting up or reading in bed. If you do give them a pillow, use a small, flat one and avoid feathers, both in case of potential allergy and also because they are difficult to wash and dry. The same thing goes for duvets. If you introduce one, keep it lightweight and easily washable.

The room temperature

The ideal room temperature for a young child is 18–21 °C (64–70 °F) – they sleep better when they are cool. Young children tend to move around a lot in their sleep and kick off their covers, so it is a good idea to put a young, nappy-aged child, to bed in a long-sleeved 'onesie' with feet, or put them in a sleep bag. For an older child, they can be taught how to replace their own covers if they come off the bed in the night, or it is possible to buy fasteners to keep a duvet in place.

The lighting

Having your child sleep in a very dark room will encourage them to sleep better. This is because darkness encourages the production of the sleep hormone, melatonin. Having too much light in the room can slow down or stop melatonin production and cause your child to be more wakeful. For this reason, it is very useful to have a blackout blind. If your child doesn't like the dark, they can have a night light. It is best to choose one with a red or orange glow, which won't affect melatonin production.

If your child falls asleep with a light on and then wakes later and it is dark, they will feel alarmed. For this reason, it is really important that the conditions and environment that your child falls asleep in remain the same all night. This applies to white noise, story tapes and parental presence, too.

Watch out for unexpected sources of light in your child's room, such as electrical devices on standby or charging. These can be a lot brighter than you think and can potentially affect their sleeping.

The ambience

In an ideal world your child's sleep space should be calm and clutter-free. Putting away their toys can be built into the bedtime routine. This ritual is great because it lets them know that it is no longer time for play. Have a rule whereby the toys must remain put away until morning, but if your child has one special toy that they take to bed with them, this is fine. Have your child's books, special toy, night-time beaker of water and anything else that they need for the night, waiting for them when they come out of the bath and into the bedroom.

It is not helpful for your child to have a TV, laptop or smartphone in their room or to fall asleep watching a screen. Even if you are supervising what they are watching, and avoiding anything scary, the blue light emitted from a screen will interfere with sleep hormone production and impair the quality of their sleep. It is far better for them to have a good-night story than to fall asleep watching something on TV.

It's lovely to think about colour schemes, co-ordinating bedding sets and furniture, but if you can provide your child with a comfortable bed in a cool, dark room, then you are doing everything you need to create the right environment to meet their sleep needs.

3

Problems with falling asleep

Not wanting to fall asleep alone

It is completely understandable that lots of young children prefer to have a parent with them when they fall asleep. Many are used to having you very close by from babyhood, when perhaps they were rocked or nursed to sleep. For some, wanting you to stay with them is a new thing that's arisen out of their natural development, when they begin to be scared of things. They may be experiencing or just getting over a period of separation anxiety, or they may simply be asserting their independence and exercising their choices. You want your child to settle to sleep feeling loved and happy, and especially if you've been out at work all day, you don't want them to feel pushed away.

For lots of children, falling asleep with a parent next to them, either in your bed or you sitting beside their bed (or in their bed) is not a problem. They drift off to sleep in a few minutes and then sleep through the night. For many others, it is not that simple, as we discovered when we talked earlier about sleep associations. Most children who are 'over-helped' to go to sleep, and then left alone, will wake up later and feel upset that you're not there anymore. In order to fall back to sleep, they need you to help them again, and if your way of managing this is to bring them into your bed or you to go and lay on the floor next to their bed or cot, they will often feel compelled to fulfil that waking ritual in the night.

Insight

Your toddler might fall asleep happily in their own bed, but if they are expecting at some point to get into your bed, they might wake often in the night to check if it's time to come to you yet. It may be that you bring them in only after 5 a.m., but, as little ones, they don't know that rule! Remember, they can't tell the time, they don't know how long they've been asleep for or how close to morning it is.

As we know, when children fall asleep, they don't *stay* asleep, at least, they don't remain in the same level of deep unconsciousness. It is normal to wake a few times in the night with the sleep cycles, and sleep is very light and broken from about 4 a.m. onwards. The important thing to realize is that they don't usually wake up because they are sad, scared or in any kind of discomfort. They wake up because it is *normal* to do so, and only then do they feel that things aren't as they should be. So, if your child falls asleep in your bed, on the sofa or in a car seat, and wakes later to find themselves in their own bed, they will quite understandably feel unsettled and confused. Or if they fall asleep in their own bed but expect later to come to yours, they will often spend the night feeling that they're in the wrong place.

For that reason, it is really good to help them fall asleep in the same conditions that they will find themselves in when they naturally wake in their sleep later on and to maintain those same conditions all night.

And the bottom line is that, unless you have made a conscious decision to bed-share or room-share, if you want your child to sleep happily through the night, you will need to help them to fall asleep supported but ultimately – deep breath – *alone*.

The deep breath is because lots of parents worry that leaving their child to settle alone will be too traumatic or rejecting, or that their child is just not capable of sleeping alone and they will stay awake all night. The fact is, though, that your child is *biologically programmed* to sleep at bedtime, and with your help, they actually *can* do it!

Case study

Two-year-old boy, Luke, only able to fall asleep with a parent next to him, and then gets into the parental bed during the night.

The situation

Luke was just over two years old and had an older brother, who was nearly four and had no sleep problems. He was already sleeping in a little bed rather than a cot because he had climbed out of his cot. His parents had a safety gate in his doorway to prevent him wandering around when he woke in the night. He needed one of them to lie with him to go to sleep at bedtime, and then he woke up later and got into their bed, so that they could all get some sleep. In fact, because Luke (like all little ones) was very active in his sleep and took over the whole bed, his parents really did not sleep well, and they woke up still feeling very tired in the morning. They were finding it tough looking after two very small children, and one of them was also in full-time paid work.

The solution

Luke's parents needed to understand that, if they helped him to fall asleep in his own bed, and to overcome the expectation of the ritual transfer to their bed, he would be more able to join together his sleep cycles, feel much more settled, and sleep the night in his own bed. They needed to approach this in a way that would be supportive and encouraging, but would also need to be consistent, determined and support one another.

Luke had the potential to be a very good sleeper but was being held back by his reliance on having one of his parents close by as he went to sleep. He then woke up in the night, was upset that they were no longer there, and felt compelled to follow the ritual of coming to their bed.

They needed to alter the routine slightly, put *themselves* in control, and help Luke to feel safe falling asleep without having them with him. They would most likely take a step or two backwards before seeing some progress, and they needed to be prepared for this.

The sleep plan

- Follow your usual preparation for bed routine with both boys together.
- Throughout the routine you should be nicely in charge, so instead of asking 'Shall we have your bath now?' or 'Do you want to get out now?' you should say, 'Come on! Bath time!' and 'Out you get, Luke!'
- Once he's dressed and has had the ritual of a drink and a story, you should kiss him good night and leave the room on a very positive note, 'I'm going to do some jobs and I'll be back to see you in a couple of minutes.' Leave the room with confidence. Stay nearby but out of his line of vision.
- Return to him within a minute or two, whether he cries/calls you or not, and praise him warmly if he has stayed in his bed.
- If he's out of bed and at the gate, go and take him back. If he won't get back into bed, don't fight with him. Just say, 'Go to bed in a few minutes then', and then leave.
- Return to him every two minutes to get him back into bed/tell him to go to bed/to praise him for being in bed if he's in it!
- When you go to him, be brief and affectionate but do not allow yourself to be drawn into any long conversations, explanations or negotiations. Just reassure him that he's OK and that it's now time for sleep.
- If he asks for anything or tries to delay you leaving, you need to respond by saying, 'We'll do that/get that/talk about that *in the morning.*'
- What is most important is that you are not only engaged with him, offering him eye contact and speaking kindly, but also *utterly consistent* and calmly resolved in your manner.
- He will eventually fall asleep because he is biologically programmed to do so. It might take a couple of hours – or longer. When he does go to sleep, make sure that you're not in the room with him.
- If he falls asleep at the gate, lift him into his bed – even if this wakes him up.
- Then each time he wakes during the night or any time before 6 a.m. and calls for you, go and reassure him but don't bring him to your bed or get into his.
- Tell him that it is still sleepy time and remind him that he is going to stay in his own bed. You should be resolute but not cross.

- Do the exits and returns as you did earlier – leaving him at the gate if you need to. You may be up more than once, and your response has to be completely consistent each time.
- If he doesn't go back to sleep, just get him up any time after 6 a.m. You will need to open his curtains first or turn the light on first to demonstrate that now it is daytime.
- Bring him into the living room rather than to your room, as this may be confusing for him, then warmly welcome him to the day. Find some aspect of his sleeping that has been good and immediately reward him with *specific* praise: 'You went to sleep all by yourself/ stayed in bed until the morning/went back to bed when I asked you to!' Give him lots of cuddles.

The outcome

The first night was tough for everyone. It took 90 minutes to fall asleep, and at times his parents thought that he was going to fall asleep standing at the gate. It was hard for them to stick with the plan, especially when Luke was asking for cuddles and for them to stay. However, they did stick with it, and even though Luke didn't fall asleep happily on that first night, his parents made sure that he did fall asleep alone in his bed, but knowing that they were close by.

He woke up twice in the night, the first time for 45 minutes, and his parents repeated the actions and responses that they had used earlier at bedtime. The second time, he was awake for 20 minutes and got up three or four times before going to sleep. In the morning he was praised and hugged and cuddled a lot.

On the second night he settled at bedtime within 20 minutes and was less upset. He woke twice, for about 10 minutes each time, and easily resettled in his bed. He was praised again in the morning.

On the third night, he settled very easily and *happily*, with his parents still popping in to praise him and reassure him that they were close by. He slept through the night and everyone woke up feeling well rested.

Conclusion

It is possible to help toddlers and young children to fall asleep by themselves, even if it seems like they will never be able to do it. The power is in your hands, and you can help your child in a way that is supportive and encouraging. Sleep is so important for their physical and mental health, and contrary to the school of thought that tells you that letting your child fall asleep alone is detrimental to their mental health, good sleep is actually beneficial to it.

Bedtime fears and anxiety

Bedtime fears or waking up in the night feeling frightened are very common in toddlers and young children. They are a natural part of a child's cognitive development as they get older, and when they begin to realize that there are things out there that could harm them. These fears affect more than half of four to six-year-olds, so they can certainly be considered as normal.

Toddlers and younger children, too, can experience fears about bedtime, but these fears are less rooted in imaginary scenarios. They tend instead to be about things in their immediate environment like a sudden noise, or Mummy or Daddy getting up and leaving them. Age is important when it comes to the type of bedtime fear that a child has. So a younger child is likely to worry about scary monsters, dragons and other creatures of their imagination or seen in books and films. Older children's fears, on the other hand, tend to be based on realistic things such as burglars, scary people, bad things happening to the family, and so on. Although these fears are normal, stress levels in the home can makes things worse for a child. This is because an anxious parent or a tense atmosphere can cause them to feel emotional or worried, even before bedtime.

Sometimes fears, scary thoughts and worries can lead a child into a feeling of **separation anxiety**, or fear of being left alone. It can be tricky to work out if your child is truly scared or if their resistance to go to bed is due to other things such as delayed sleep onset, or just simply resisting bedtime because they are enjoying playing, or watching TV. Children quickly come to realize that, if they say they are scared, you are more likely to be sympathetic, than if they say they that don't want to go to bed because they are playing a game. Naturally, you should give them the benefit of the doubt, and if they say that they are scared, they need you to respond in the right way. That way may not necessarily mean staying beside them as they go to sleep, however.

Importantly, studies have shown that there are lots of children who feel scared at bedtime or in the night, but don't tell their parents. So if your child is not crying, clinging on to you at bedtime or telling you that they are frightened, what are the hidden signs to look out for that your child is feeling scared about going to sleep? There are many, but these are the main ones:

- saying they're not tired
- telling you that they feel poorly – and actually feeling poorly sometimes, with tummy ache/upset or headaches
- delaying tactics such as needing a drink/feeling hungry/not having the right pyjamas on
- curtain calls – where they are basically coming to find you and check that you're still there and/or hoping that you'll come and stay with them as they go to sleep
- sleeping better when they occasionally share a room with someone else (on holiday, for example).

Of course, many of these signs can be typical of a tired child who is just testing the limits. If your child is resisting bedtime but also tends to be oppositional with other things that are not sleep-related, then their night-time behaviour is probably just part of a bigger picture of how they are at the moment. Whether your child is genuinely scared at bedtime or simply pushing against the boundaries, your approach to dealing with it is going to be exactly the same – calm and kind with a gentle authority which will let them know that they are safe. And the good thing is that, if you can handle bedtime fears and resistance in a positive way, you will be better able to help them with tricky daytime behaviours too.

Let's start with putting a child to bed who is scared of being alone. I'm going to give you some dos and don'ts, and I'll start with the don'ts!

Don't...

- look under your child's bed/wardrobe/windowsill to check that there are no monsters there;
- use imaginary monster killer spray in the room before they go to sleep;
- tell them things that give truth to the existence of fictitious creatures, such as 'No bad fairies are coming tonight because we haven't invited them!' or 'Mummy and Daddy will keep the dragons away from you!';
- sit or lie beside them, or sit inside or just outside their room as they go to sleep;
- let them have a screen device in their bed to distract them.

The first three of these strategies, while they might help in the short term, will only tell a child that their fears are real and that you believe them, too. Otherwise why *would* you be checking under the bed and staying with them for protection? Screens in bed are a really bad idea, as they delay sleep onset and impair the quality of their sleep, by restricting the production of the sleep hormone, melatonin.

Do...

- listen to their fears and show them that you care about how they feel;
- explain that monsters/bad fairies and so on are pretend and are only in books, films and other fictional situations;
- let them know, if they are old enough to understand, that night-time worrying is normal for children;
- demonstrate to them that they are in your safe hands;
- tell them over and over that you are close by, can hear them, will keep them safe and nothing bad will happen;
- encourage them to repeat positive statements such as 'I am safe in my bed!' '*I'm* not scared!' 'Monsters are not in real life!' Get them to say these statements *out loud*;

- let them have a night light on/their bedroom door semi-open/a touch light/torch or similar. Nightlights should be red, to encourage melatonin production;
- leave their bedroom door open a little bit, so they know you can hear them;
- encourage comfort/transitional objects such as a favourite teddy or blanket;
- allow room sharing with a sibling(s) if that's practical and works for you;
- consider allowing a (quiet) pet in the bedroom if they think it would help (a pet *not* like my youngest daughter's hamster whose whizzing round on its wheel kept the whole family up in the night);
- look at some of the wonderfully reassuring children's books available which address and help with bedtime fears. A good example is Paulette Bourgeois's *Franklin in the Dark* (Kids Can Press, 2014);
- avoid scary stories – especially at bedtime;
- as much as you can, supervise what they see on TV or hear on the radio, and be aware that sometimes news programmes will broadcast material that can be upsetting for young children. If they do see or hear anything distressing, make sure that you take time to talk about it and put it into context, for example, 'The reason that that has made it onto TV is because things like that happen so rarely' or 'Things like that don't happen in our street';
- teach an older child some simple relaxation/distraction techniques;
- tell them to stay in their bed and that you will go in and check them regularly. Do go back reliably and frequently, rather than have them leave the room to find you. If they call out for you, call back and let them know you'll be coming to them soon. When you do go back, always praise them for waiting;
- give rewards in the morning for sleeping alone, staying in their bed or being brave;
- encourage them to talk about their fears. Talking will make things feel better rather than worse. Listen and reassure them but don't reinforce or give truth to their fear. Respond with something like, 'That's a scary thing that you're thinking, and I'm not surprised that you don't want to be on your own, but nothing bad like that can ever happen to you here, and it's safe for you to go to sleep.'

This last point is important, because many parents think that, if they engage in a discussion about their child's fears, they will encourage the fears to continue. This isn't true, although *over-reassuring* can sometimes give credence to fears of things that are very unlikely to happen. On the whole, don't be scared to talk to your child about their worries. It's fine to bring up the subject and encourage them to say out loud the things that are frightening/worrying them. Even if you can't completely remove the fear, the very fact of saying it out loud will help.

If their thoughts are based on their own imagination, get them to describe the images to you and then help them change them to less threatening ones. So if they imagine a man with a knife/a monster dripping with blood, tell them that, with their imaginary magic wand or superpower, they can change that picture to a kind man with a bunch of flowers/a beautiful horse dripping with raindrops ... and so on. This technique also helps when they have a scary dream.

With an older child, if their thoughts and fears are grounded in reality, for example of possible intruders/burglars and similar, you can still help them to replace the bad thought with a good thought, and then speak the thought aloud. So teach them to *say out loud*, 'That's just the neighbour putting something in his bin' or 'That's only the stairs creaking – you'd creak if you'd been walked on all day!' If they say it a few times, it will become a new and less frightening thought.

Also, as a parent, it might help you to recognize that it is the *thought* in your child's head that causes the *feeling* of fear. If you can help them to change the thought, you can ease their unwanted feeling.

On a very practical note, with all young children who are scared at bedtime, it is important not to put them to bed too early. If they go to bed with energy to spare, they will spend that time worrying. With most young children, a huge build-up of sleep pressure, leading to extreme sleepiness will *override* fear and anxiety, and if you can get them into the habit of getting into bed and falling to sleep quickly, even if at first it is at a time that you consider to be way too late for them, you can then gradually bring their bedtime forward when they start to fall asleep easily and within a few minutes of going to bed. Look at the following case study as an example of what I mean.

Case study
Four-year-old boy, James, scared of monsters at bedtime, put to bed in his own bed but only able to fall asleep very late at night, ultimately in his mum's bed, with her beside him.

The situation
James had always had problems with his sleep, and when he was a baby he was only ever able to sleep at night by being rocked or fed to sleep by his mum.

When I met the family, he was finding it very difficult to fall asleep without his mum next to him (he wouldn't accept his dad), and despite being put to bed at 7 p.m., he would remain awake, getting up and coming to find his mum, until after 9 p.m. most nights. He would tell her that he was scared of monsters and wait for her to eventually, out of desperation, bring him to her own bed and lie with him until he went to sleep. Once he was asleep, she would carry him through to his own bed, only for him to wake later, feeling very upset, and come back to her bed.

James was a generally happy boy in the daytime, with no obvious general anxiety, who was developing typically and enjoying full-time preschool nursery (both parents worked full time).

The solution
To resolve James' sleep problem, which was affecting the whole family, his parents needed to help him feel happy and secure falling asleep in his own bed, and to recognize his bed as a safe place in which he stayed for the duration of the night. He was welcome to come into their bed for a cuddle in the morning after 7 a.m.

The first part of the sleep plan was to put him to bed only when he was *very* tired and to support him to fall asleep in his own bed. Then, once he was able to fall asleep alone within 20 minutes of his mum kissing him good night, his bedtime could be brought forward by 15 minutes each week, provided he was still falling asleep within 20 minutes of the earlier bedtime. If at any time during the process he started taking a long time to fall asleep again, they would stop bringing bedtime forward and instead push it later by 15 minutes until he started falling asleep more quickly and with less distress.

He was to be woken up each morning by 8 a.m. if he hadn't woken by himself and he was not to take any naps.

The ultimate goal was for him to fall asleep happily and alone in his own bed at around 7 p.m., but for the family to accept it if his ideal bedtime actually turned out to be a bit later than this.

The sleep plan

- Get a digital clock with a red display and cover up all but the second number. When James sees the number 7 on the clock (7 a.m. onwards), that is when he can come into your bed.
- If he sleeps beyond 7 a.m., wake him up just before 8 a.m. (while the 7 is still on the clock) and tell him that it is getting-up time.
- Avoid any daytime naps.
- When you are ready to make a start, tell James that tonight he is going to *stay up late* and then sleep in his own bed. Tell him that you are going to help him. Explain that, in the night, he will be staying in his own bed and not getting into yours, but you will leave his and your bedroom doors open and you will be able to hear him.
- James currently takes a long time to fall asleep. When he gets into his bed at night he doesn't *expect* to go sleep right away; in fact, bedtime is his cue for him to start getting worried, thinking about monsters, and getting out of bed to find you.
- The best way to tackle this is to put him to bed *very* close to the time that he's naturally falling asleep right now. The increase in sleep pressure and sleepiness will make his fears less severe. Then, once he starts to fall asleep more quickly and with less distress or fear, you can gradually bring his bedtime forward.
- So given that he currently falls asleep at 9 p.m., let him stay up and play until 8.30 p.m. Avoid having him lying down or watching TV in case he falls asleep on the sofa.
- At 8.30 p.m., offer him a simple snack of fruit, toast or cereal before taking him for a bath or shower. During this time talk to him about how monsters are only in books and films, and tell him that other children worry about them, too!
- He needs a bath or shower every night just before bed, then take him directly from the bathroom to his own bed and tuck him in. Then finish the day off with a new ritual, 'What was the best thing that happened today?'

- After this, tell him to snuggle down and get cosy – turn any big lights off but keep the door semi open and have a low bathroom or corridor light on, if he wants this. There will also be a bit of light from his clock. By now it will be about 9 p.m.
- Tell him that you are going to do some jobs but that you'll listen out for him and come back to check him in two minutes. 'Good night, James. I'm going to do my jobs but I'll be back in a few minutes. Stay in your bed!' Leave the room with confidence and go out of his line of vision.
- Return to him in two minutes, whether he cries/calls you or not, and praise him warmly if he has stayed quietly in his bed. It is better that you are choosing to return to him rather than being called for. Once you have shown him that, when you say you'll come back, you *will* come back, you can tell him that you'll be checking on him again in two minutes.
- Each time that you go to him, only stay for a few seconds to praise him for waiting and staying in his bed. Keep conversation to a minimum.
- If he says that he is frightened of burglars or monsters, tell him again that monsters are only in books and films and that he is safe in his bed.
- **If he calls out for you**, call back and tell him that you'll be there in two minutes.
- **If he gets out of bed and comes to the door**, you should greet him with a 'surprised' response: 'What are you doing up?!' Quickly and quietly take him back to bed. Be calm, not cross, when you do this. Stay with him for a just a few moments to tell him that he needs to stay in bed while you are doing jobs.
- **If he continually gets up or struggles to go back to bed or stay in bed**, rather than giving up and lying down with him or bringing him to your bed, go into his room with him and close the door behind you. Stand still, facing him and calmly say, 'James, go back to bed.' Just say it once and then wait ... for as long it takes. Don't have any other conversation, other than to say, 'Come on now, James.' The only exception would be if he wants to go to the toilet, in which case, he can go and then come and get back into bed. Otherwise, just wait, standing quietly in his room until he feels compelled to go back to bed (which he will do). When this happens, you should praise him warmly: 'That's brilliant, James! I'm so glad that you're getting back into bed. I know this isn't easy, but you're doing so

well!' Once he's back in his bed, tell him that you will still keep coming back every two minutes.

- On that first night or two, he might still take as long to fall asleep and it is not likely that he will fall into a happy sleep, but this is temporary and he'll soon learn how to fall asleep more quickly and be more content falling asleep in his own bed without you lying next to him. Don't worry that he has fallen asleep out of exhaustion rather than choice. **The aim right now is just to change his sleep behaviour, and the happy feelings will follow later.**
- If he wakes during the night – no matter how many times before 7 a.m. and calls for you, you need to call back from your room for him to snuggle down and stay in his bed. If he comes to your room, you (Mummy, *not* Daddy) need to take him back to his own bed. If Daddy does this on the first few nights, James will feel like Daddy is blocking him from Mummy.
- If he gets upset, you can go to him and tell him it is still night-time. Listen and reassure him if he says that he's scared/lonely and so on, but let that come from him. Don't be the one to ask what is wrong, or he may think that something *should* be wrong, or even feel as if he needs to think of something! Tell him that you can hear him and will see him in the morning. You should be resolute but not angry, and if you need to, you can stand in his room, as you may have done earlier, quietly waiting for him to go back to bed and praising him when he does so.
- If he remains awake and upset, return every two minutes to reassure him and repeat the message. If he doesn't go back to sleep, just get him up any time after 7 a.m. Before you do this, you will need to remark that the 7 is on the clock.
- You can now welcome him to the day, and praise what he has achieved, 'You went to sleep all by yourself!' or 'You went back to bed when I asked you to!' or 'You stayed in your bed all last night!' Reinforce the praise with a piece of pasta to collect in an empty jar. When his jar is full, he can have a prize (a special outing/cooking the pasta that he has collected/a toy that he wants, etc.)
- After a week, if he is falling asleep alone within 20 minutes, you can start to bring his bedtime forward by 15 minutes every two nights, provided that he still falls asleep within 20 minutes. If he starts taking longer or getting very upset, then do a 15-minutes-later bedtime again until things are easier for him, and then restart the gradual process of bringing his bedtime forward.

- His ideal settling time may be more like 7.30 p.m. now that he's a bit older, but you'll soon find out by how long it takes for him to fall asleep.
- Once you have established happier and earlier bedtimes, it is time to help James accept his dad putting him to bed at night. Keep the pasta reward jar going, and add a bonus piece each time Daddy puts him to bed.

The outcome
On the first night, despite the earlier bedtime, James still cried and took just as long to fall asleep. He got up twice instead of his usual six to eight times, and he fell asleep alone at just after 10 p.m. He woke at 1 a.m. and took 40 minutes to go back to sleep, but he did so in his own bed. He woke just after 7 a.m. and was welcomed into his parents' bed and given lots of praise. His mum said that, even though it was a difficult night, she felt confident and in control. She was reassured to see that, on the following day, James was his usual happy self.

The family followed the sleep plan, with the 9 p.m. bedtime for the first week, and then, because James was falling asleep more quickly, they began bringing bedtime forward in 15-minute increments. Within three weeks, with a few tricky nights along the way, James was going to bed at 7 p.m., falling asleep within 15 minutes and sleeping through the night in his own bed until morning. His parents were alternating putting him to bed, and both of them felt that James was much happier in the daytime once he had increased his hours of sleep. Overall, the quality of life for all of them was much better now that they were having happier bedtimes and getting more sleep.

Conclusion
It is possible to handle children's bedtime and night-time fears sensitively and *effectively* using practical techniques. It takes confidence and a bit of effort to make a plan and stick to it, but if you can do it, you will all benefit in the long run.

Lying beside your child until they go to sleep may inadvertently reinforce their fears, and having them wake up with you no longer beside them can cause them to panic. So, unless you have made a conscious decision to co-sleep, it is better for them if you can help them to fall asleep in their own bed.

Putting them to bed very late (in technical terms, this is called sleep restriction/bedtime restriction) might feel wrong to you, but it is a recognized, safe and effective technique if used as a temporary measure, and a means to an end.

Taking a long time to fall asleep

Many parents who know that it takes their child a long time to fall asleep will put them to bed very early, with the intention of giving them the time they need to go through the usual curtain calls, procrastinations and negotiations before eventually falling asleep. Although that approach might seem to make sense, it actually compounds the problem and leads to a situation, as in the example with James, above, whereby a child goes to bed *and doesn't expect to go to sleep.*

As we saw in Chapter 2, young children are naturally ready to settle down for the night usually between 6 and 8 p.m. If you remember, to help them settle, they need to have a build-up of sleep pressure and they also need to be producing plenty of melatonin, the sleep hormone. However, as we know, sometimes behavioural factors can override or interfere with biological ones, and if a child has built up a very strong association with getting into bed and not being able to sleep, then, even if they are very tired, they will struggle to get to sleep!

So why does this sleep delay happen? Here are the main reasons:

- bedtime fears and anxiety
- delay in the production of melatonin
- napping – too long, too late or when they're too old for a nap *and* an early bedtime
- testing the limits and boundaries.

In the previous section we looked at how fears and anxieties about specific threats can cause children to be so worried that they can't sleep alone and often experience significant delay in getting off to sleep. There are lots of children, however, particularly when they are moving away from toddlerhood and are in the preschool age range, who aren't especially scared of stuff, but their worry is that **they won't be able to go to sleep.** When this happens, it can become self-fulfilling – they get into bed and think, 'Oh no! I can't sleep!' This situation is often made worse or even caused by truly caring parents, who unwittingly put too much pressure on their child by telling them how important it is that they sleep, saying 'If you don't go to sleep soon, you'll be tired in the morning' or 'I have a busy day at work tomorrow and I need you to fall asleep now.' This kind of reasoning rarely helps children to fall asleep, and it can make them feel guilty or stressed.

Tips to help your child if they are worried that they can't get to sleep

- Put them to bed at the time that they usually fall asleep (which may be significantly later than their usual bedtime), and once they are falling asleep within 20 minutes, bring their bedtime forward by 15 minutes every two nights until you find their ideal bedtime.
- Rather than telling them to go to sleep, instead ask them to snuggle down/get cosy/and similar. Reassure them that sleep will come eventually, and that they can relax and let their body rest.
- With an older child, give them a little mental exercise to do that may help to focus their mind away from the task of going to sleep. Ask them to close their eyes and count five things in each of the following categories – animals, dinosaurs, foods and vehicles. You can add more categories according to your child's interests and age.
- With a younger child, it's OK to have a gentle audio story to listen to as they drift off, but you *may* then have to have this playing at a low volume on a loop all night. This is so that they don't feel there's something missing when they naturally wake up in their sleep.

- If they are in the habit of getting up and looking for you at bedtime, it is better that you go to them rather than them coming to you, so, within the context of the temporarily later bedtime, which will make them much sleepier and act somewhat as a 'reset', you can also try popping in and out to them 2–5 minutes – 'Just checking that you're cosy!' – and reassuring them if they're worried about not being able to sleep.
- It is better that children who worry about not being able to go to sleep do not have a clock in their room, as this can often add to their worries and become a bit of an unhelpful focus. A simple sleep training clock, which doesn't actually tell the time, but rather lets them know when it's OK to get up, is fine to have in the room – provided that if the daytime signifier is a light changing colour, the continuous night light or "sleep mode" is not a blue light!
- If your child does not seem to be anxious about getting to sleep and hasn't expressed any fears about monsters or other things, but still takes a long time to go to sleep, there are a few very practical things that you can do to help them. The most important thing is to really encourage the plentiful production of their natural sleep hormone, melatonin. Here are some ways of doing this:
  - Exposure to daylight, especially pre-noon, will set your child's internal circadian clock to sleep at night and increase their melatonin production.
  - Keep your child's bedroom as dark as possible, but if they need a night light, choose a dim one with a red glow.
  - Avoid too much screen time, particularly in the evening before bed. Lots of children will watch a little bit of gentle TV after dinner, almost as the beginning of their bedtime routine, and this is fine, but do make a point of turning all screens off at least half an hour before bedtime.
  - Don't let them take a screen device to bed with them for distraction. It will only keep them awake for longer.
  - Recent research has suggested that having a warm bath promotes the production of melatonin, but even if it doesn't, it is still a great sleep cue.
  - Give your child food which is rich in tryptophan, such as milk, cheese, tuna, turkey and bananas! **Tryptophan** is an amino acid which helps to make **serotonin** (another sleep hormone and a 'feel good' hormone) as well as melatonin.

If your child is coming up to the age of three and can only settle to sleep at a reasonable time when they haven't had a nap, and yet, without the nap, they are exhausted and tearful before bedtime, then you are in something of a dilemma. Be assured that this tricky period won't last for long, and they will soon build up enough stamina to be able to miss the nap and make it till bedtime. Until they do, you will need to consider having two different bedtimes – a 6 p.m. (or as close to it as you can) bedtime when they haven't napped and an 8 p.m. bedtime when they have.

Yes, I know I have advised you that a regular bedtime is important for a child's sleep, and to a large extent this is true, but respecting their own timing is also very important. It's not fair to push a child on to their 'set' bedtime when they haven't napped and are on their little knees with exhaustion. Neither is it helpful to put them to bed when have napped and they are not tired enough to sleep again – this, as we know, can lead to bedtime resistance and set up behaviour patterns like procrastination and curtain calls, which often then tend to stick!

While it's fine to vary the bedtime according to whether they have napped or not, it is good to encourage some regularity by waking them at roughly the same time each morning – if they haven't woken up of their own accord – and then getting them out in the morning to benefit from that morning light exposure!

Finally, one of the most common reasons why children resist going to sleep at bedtime is simply because they don't want to. They don't want to stop what they are doing, and the fun they are having. They may be sufficiently tired and biologically ready to sleep, and they may have had a lovely, familiar bedtime routine, but *because* they are tired, they are struggling with controlling their emotions around being made to 'switch off' for the day.

This is where the bit about loving boundaries that I mentioned in Chapter 2 really comes into its own. Letting your child know what the boundaries are, without telling them off or making them feel humiliated, is the best possible way to manage bedtime resistance and challenging behaviour. Bedtime is the time of day when the way that you communicate with your child really matters most. Unfortunately, it is also the time of day, when your own energy levels are dropping and you might not be feeling able to be super positive.

Let me help by emphasizing the tips that I gave in Chapter 2 and adding a few more suggestions:

- Have a few minutes of precious 'you and me' time, spent cuddling/reading or chatting together, before starting the bedtime routine. You might have to share this with more than one child, but it will still be lovely!
- Follow a predictable bedtime routine with a clear and recognizable series of steps leading up to bedtime.
- The sequence is more important than the timing, so start the routine about half an hour before you feel your child is ready to sleep rather than having a time that's set in stone.
- Don't let your child become overtired (unless you are dealing with sleep onset delay or bed time fears and are following my advice from the previous section), as this makes them even less able to manage their emotions and makes it more likely they will have a tantrum.
- Give them warnings about what's happening next – for example 'Five more minutes drawing and then it's bath time.'
- Give directions rather than ask questions. Think of yourself as a kind and loving authority figure – one who values them, gives guidance, encouragement and credit where it's due, and is always straight and honest with them.
- Don't ask your child to do more than one thing at a time. Saying, 'Put your toys away, come for your bath and bring your teddy' is *too much*!
- Start with 'Put your toys away, my love' then stand quietly, watch and wait until they move towards doing it. It might

take a while for them to do as you ask, but try just waiting it out, standing very still and *not* continuously repeating the instruction. As soon as they start to move towards picking up a toy, you can start the warm praise, saying something like 'Brilliant! What lovely tidying!'

- If you haven't got time to wait, then you can say, 'I can help you, then.' Tidy up together and praise them when they put something away. Try not to behave in a cross and sulky way that mirrors their own behaviour. Remember that you are the grown-up and you are in charge.

- If they have a tantrum, realize that tantrums are a normal part of their development at this age, and it is not their fault. Stay quiet but present until it passes over, then give them a cuddle, reassure them that they are OK and carry on with the routine.

- During any bedtime tantrums don't raise your voice over theirs; if you start shouting, your child will feel even more out of control. Don't ask them any questions, or try to appease them with suggestions like 'Do you need a different toy/a drink/a biscuit?' If they are having a tantrum because you've said that they can't have something or do something, do not give in and give them what they want. If you do this, you will teach them that having a tantrum is the way to getting what they want.

- However, if they are not having a tantrum but simply don't want to have a bath/clean their teeth/put their pyjamas on, it's OK, so long as *you feel in charge* and say, 'Just have a little paddle in the water then' or 'Just a lick of the toothpaste, then, tonight!' or 'OK, a nappy and cuddly blanket it is!' This might look like giving in, but another way of looking at it is as you granting permission. Quite honestly, with little children, you need to ask yourself how much their refusal to toe the line in a particular situation really matters. If their refusal is about something relatively minor, then, rather than having an unnecessary battle at the end of which they are humiliated and you feel awful, it is better sometimes to accept their refusal with grace, as the kind and loving adult. You are there to guide them and nurture them, but you don't want to be constantly on their case, denying their individual preferences.

- Remember always that you are the adult, and try not to respond to them as an equal. If they hit or bite you, they are struggling with their feelings. Don't hit or bite them back as a way of showing them how it feels to be hit or bitten. It is much better to tell them that you don't want them to hit or bite you. Restrain them from doing it again, telling them, 'You must be feeling very upset if you want to bite me.' Recognize that it is just them feeling tired/overwhelmed/ frustrated.
- Young children struggle with stopping one activity and moving on to another. You'll see this difficulty played out many times during the day, and bedtime is often the toughest transition of the day. This is the case for children and parents alike, and if you can be the leader, keeping them safe and guiding them, then their bedtime will be calmer, quicker and more enjoyable.

4

Night-time sleep problems

Night waking

So far, we have mainly talked about getting your child to bed and helping them how to fall asleep. In many ways, helping a child to *fall asleep* well, is the most important thing to concentrate on. The reason for this is that if they fall asleep at bedtime happily and independently, they are then very likely to sleep through the night, joining their sleep cycles and waking up in the morning feeling well rested, happy to see you and ready to take on the day!

I sometimes sense that parents get frustrated during a consultation with me when I focus on how their child falls asleep at bedtime, and will tell me that falling asleep at bedtime is not the problem; it's the waking up that they are worried about. I usually explain that it is *how* their child falls asleep which determines how well they will sleep at night. They may well fall asleep happily at bedtime with Daddy lying down on the floor next to them, but then there is every chance that they'll wake later and be upset that he's not there anymore.

However, it's not that uncommon for a child to put themselves to sleep completely independently at bedtime, but *still* wake in the night, looking to get into their parent's or parents' bed or have them come to sleep with them or on their floor. Of course, all children will need a parent or carer from time to time in the night if they are poorly or have had a bad dream for example, but if this happens every night, then the chances are that your child might be seeking you out of habit, as part of their nightly ritual. It's a shame if this happens, as there will be times when your child wakes in the night and just wants to go back to sleep, but feels *compelled* to come and find you, because 'This is what I do!'

It's possible to break this habit and help your child and you to get through the night peacefully and without any unnecessary rituals.

Here's a case study that shows how toddlers can become hooked on night-time rituals.

Case study
Two-year-old girl, Eleanor, putting herself to sleep without help at bedtime but waking in the night to get into bed with her parents.

The situation
Eleanor was a healthy, typically developing two-year-old with an older brother, Theo, who was five years old. She had a regular nap of one and a half hours every day after lunch and was ready to sleep for the night by 7 p.m. Her family had a very good bedtime routine and Eleanor always settled by herself in her own cot. But every night, she woke up around midnight and cried until she was brought to her parents' bed. One parent would then go and sleep on the sofa.

Often, a ritual of getting into the parents' bed in the night happens because this is where the child has originally fallen asleep at bedtime. Sometimes, it is because a parent has been with the child in their own room as they have gone to sleep, and they don't want to sit there again during the night. In Eleanor's case, neither of these things was happening. She didn't need a parent to be next to her as she fell asleep, but she was in the habit of getting into their bed in the night. It was as if she considered her own cot to be merely a 'holding pen'.

The solution
Eleanor's parents needed to stop the nightly ritual of transferring her to their bed and help her to recognize her cot as not just a temporary resting place, but as a safe and permanent place where she would stay for the duration of the night.

To make things easier for her, they were to make some changes to her routine at her bedtime that would challenge her established settling skills and engineer a little bit of protest from her.

They would then set in place a response to Eleanor, which (because this is the start of the night) would necessarily culminate in her falling asleep quite easily in her cot, despite the changes. Then, when she woke at her usual time in the night, this same response could be used again, to help her fall back to sleep in her cot rather than in their bed. This is a far better approach than attempting to tackle the problem when she woke in the night, after she had already had about five hours of sleep. In other words, she would be doing the learning at bedtime, when she was naturally most able to fall asleep and then, when she woke in the night, her parents would be reinforcing something that she had *already* learned.

The sleep plan

- Follow your usual bedtime routine but instead of bringing Eleanor downstairs after her bath, take her directly to her room.
- Explain to her brother Theo that you're teaching Eleanor how to sleep in her own bed, and he might hear her 'being cross'. Reassure him that you will be staying with her and helping her.
- Give her milk in her bedroom with the curtains open/light kept on and discourage her from getting too dozy on it by looking at books together.
- Afterwards, introduce one final book to look at together which will be the same one each night until her sleep problems have resolved.
- Then have a new ritual of going to the window, saying good night to the world, and closing the curtains together. When you've done this, kiss her good night and put her into her cot. The change in the routine should make her more wakeful, but put her into her cot regardless. Do not wait for her to appear sleepy.
- If she is OK in the cot, you can potter in and out of her room, repeating a sleepy mantra such as 'Time to sleep now, Eleanor!' each time you go in to her.
- When she cries (which is quite likely) instead of popping in and out, you can kneel down beside her cot. She is likely to be standing up, so make sure that her cot base is set at its lowest level, to prevent her climbing out.
- Then with the cot side between you, you can hold and cuddle her as she is standing. Do not force her into her sleeping position but, every 2–3 minutes or so, you can encourage her to lie down. If she gets up or won't let you lay her down, you should wait for another 2–3 minutes or so before trying to reposition her again.
- It is good to keep eye contact with her and repeatedly use the sleepy mantra, which she will come to recognize as a sleep signifier.

- Don't be afraid of her crying, and please be assured that she will be OK. You are kneeling right beside her, and therefore she won't be feeling frightened or abandoned.
- The reason for doing this is to reassure her that all is OK, even though you've changed her routine, and to set in place a different response from you that will inevitably culminate in her going to sleep. You will then be able to use this when she wakes during the night, at which time getting to sleep (without bringing her to your bed) is more difficult for her.
- As she eventually calms down and stays lying down, withdraw the amount of your contact, until you are sitting beside her with just your hand on her. It's OK to stay beside her until she goes to sleep.
- When Eleanor wakes later expecting the usual ritual of the transfer, you should leave her just for a few moments to see if she can settle herself. If she becomes upset, you need to go to her. Then kneel beside her, keeping her in her cot, and do exactly as you did when you first put her to bed. She will recognize your actions and words, as having been the precursor to her going to sleep earlier on. If she asks to go to your bed, you can say, 'In the morning!'
- Expect her to be awake a lot on the first night, and please just calmly stay with it. She will come to no harm, and it is perfectly OK to stay with her if she needs you. Eventually, she will run out of energy and go back to sleep.
- She may wake a few times at first, in which case be as consistent in your response as possible. It will probably be particularly difficult at 4 or 5 a.m., but please stand your ground.
- When you get her up for the day – any time after 6 a.m. and only when she is giving you clear signs that she's ready to be up – you need to open her curtains first, as a daytime signifier. put the light on, and then very cheerfully get her up and bring her to your room to start the day.
- Before you bring her through, make sure that your curtains are open and/or your bedroom light is on. Have some toys or even a little snack ready for her. This transfer to your bed should be clearly seen by her as a daytime event, not as part of her night.

Night 3 or 4 onwards
- Before starting this sleep plan, Eleanor was happily going to sleep at bedtime without you in the room with her. We need now to help her do that again. So, after following your new routine, kiss Eleanor good night, then leave the room as you used to do.

- *If she is unsettled by you leaving her,* return to her every 2 minutes or so until she starts to go to sleep. Each time you go in to her, repeat the same sleepy phrase, 'Time to sleep now, Eleanor!' and then leave again.
- It's fine to lay her down/reposition her, and it's good to have some affectionate words and eye contact and give her a little kiss, but you should spend no more than a few seconds in the room. Be brief but kind.
- Leave the room even if she is crying and standing up. If she has thrown anything out of her cot, you can leave it there for a couple of minutes; you'll soon be going back in to replace it.
- Give her as long as she needs to settle to sleep without you in the room with her.
- When her crying becomes less urgent or when she is lying down and sounding more sleepy, it is best to not go at all but rather watch her discreetly from the door or on the monitor until she settles to sleep.
- If Eleanor wakes up in the night, you should leave her until she actually calling for you and standing up. Then just as you were popping in and to her at her bedtime earlier, you should do the same now. If she's just fussing and complaining but it's for a prolonged period, it is best to just listen or watch for her rather than going in.
- The first night or two might be a bit of a challenge, but the following nights will get easier and over the next few days she will begin to sleep through until morning.

The outcome
Eleanor's parents followed the sleep plan very closely, and in less than a week, she was sleeping through the night in her own cot. She was her usual lovely self when she woke in the morning and was very happy to reunite with her parents and be welcomed to their bed. Theo also started coming into his parents' bed in the morning, whereas before he was 'banned' as they were keeping things dark and quiet to help Eleanor stay sleeping. Everyone was better rested, and both children benefitted, because their parents had more energy and were more cheerful.

It is so easy to see a child's night waking and seeking contact with you in the night as a sign that they are sad, lonely or in need of reassurance, and of course sometimes this can be the case. But if it is happening every night, these disturbed nights are more likely to be driven by habit rather than need. It is OK to change things if you're not happy with the relentless broken nights. You will not be doing your child a disservice by helping them to sleep all night in their own bed.

Waking for night-time feeds

Lots of toddlers and young children wake in the night for a bottle or a breastfeed. If you're breastfeeding and you're OK with the night-time disturbance, and if you're sure that the night feeds are not interfering with their daytime appetite for the nutrients and the calories that they need, then there is no need to stop feeding your toddler at night.

However, if your child is waking for bottles of formula when they are over a year old, or if you're breastfeeding and your child is hardly eating in the day, or is feeding on and off all night, then you might need to think about stopping the night feeds.

With both breastfeeding and formula feeding, night-time milk is about so much more than the food of course, and certainly by the time that they are toddlers, the need for the night feeds is not driven by hunger. Many parents choose to continue to breastfeed in the night until their child no longer asks for it, and this is absolutely fine, of course, especially if you feel confident about and in control of that decision. It is OK to carry on breastfeeding in the night for as long as you both like. It is also OK to stop when you've had enough – especially if the disturbed nights are affecting your functioning and your mental and/or physical wellbeing.

If ideally you *would* like to drop the night feeds now, but are scared of doing so, then let's start with me offering you a bit of reassurance. When your child is over a year old, even if they are small, provided that they are medically OK, then from a paediatric or physiological point of view, they do not need to have any night feeds. In fact, feeding at night can often lead to a vicious circle where they eat less in the day and then you worry that they will be hungry at night.

Whereas breastfed children like to fall asleep in your arms or lying beside you while nursing, some bottle-fed children enjoy falling asleep in their cot or bed, holding their own bottle and drinking the milk to put themselves to sleep. When children fall asleep drinking their milk, they usually need milk again to put themselves back to sleep when they wake naturally later. It's not because they are hungry, but rather that the action of drinking milk is their sleep cue.

Milk as we all know is very nutritious, and it contains lots of calcium for their growing bones and teeth. After the first few months of life, however, children need more than just milk to nourish them. All milk, including breast milk is very low in iron (although the iron in breast milk is easier to absorb.) This low iron content in milk doesn't matter when they are very young because, when babies are first born, they have their own inbuilt iron stores. After the first few months, this store starts to run out and they need to then take the iron that they need through their food. If a child drinks a lot of milk at night, it can some-times lead to them not eating other essential foods during the daytime.

In some extreme cases, children who drink milk to the exclusion of other food can run the risk of developing iron deficiency anaemia.

Children need about a pint of milk a day, but after the first year it should no longer be their main food. If your child has a tiny daytime appetite, you need to watch out that they are not drinking too much milk, and offer them food that is rich in both iron and vitamin C (which is needed to absorb the iron that they eat).

Symptoms of anaemia are:

- pale skin
- tiredness
- fast heartbeat

- irritability
- reduced appetite
- brittle nails
- sore or swollen tongue.

A child with mild or developing anaemia may not show these (rather vague) symptoms, so if you are concerned about your child's eating, and they show any of the above signs, you should seek advice from your GP, paediatrician or health visitor.

Another drawback of children still having night feeds is that it delays the process of night-time dryness and keeps them in nappies at night for longer. This in itself may not be a big deal, but, actually, at night-time it is good for your child's body to truly rest and repair. Having night feeds will keep their kidneys and digestive system working during the night, and this, along with the blood sugar boost and the actual *incentive* for waking that the night feeds give, all come together to reduce the quality of your child's sleeping.

Finally, with bottle-feeding babies, falling asleep with a teat in their mouth it is not good for their teeth.

As a parent you are hard-wired to nourish and nurture your child, and withholding food when they ask for it is completely counterintuitive. However, if your child's daytime appetite is poor, if mealtimes are stressful and upsetting for you and your child, and if you're up in the night providing milk feeds, then it makes sense to make some changes.

Case study
A three-year-old girl, Evie, having up to three bottles of milk in the night and not eating well in the day.

The problem
Evie was a bright and outgoing three-year-old with good language skills. When she was a new baby there had been some difficulties with getting breastfeeding going, and for a while her weight gain was slower than normal. Evie's mum, Amanda, had to take her to the

clinic for weekly weigh-ins. In the end the breastfeeding was established, and Evie's weight picked up. At just over a year, she moved from breastfeeding to having bottles of cow's milk, which she took to very well.

Amanda said that since those early days when Evie was not getting enough milk, she had a fear of her ever being hungry. Amanda's fear was totally understandable under the circumstances.

Evie did not eat well in the daytime, despite Amanda giving her lovely nutritious meals that she had made herself. She had tried sitting down and eating together and even distracting her with a tablet computer at mealtimes, but Evie still only picked at her food. She only wanted milk – and most of this she took at night.

She needed a nappy change in the night, and her morning nappy was always saturated. During the day Evie was toilet-trained and didn't wear nappies.

The solution

Amanda needed to understand that the early feeding problems may have led to a reluctance to drop Evie's night feeds. She might want to consider talking to someone about that difficult time.

She needed to drop the night bottles now so that Evie's body could properly rest at night-time and would have a better appetite for her daytime meals.

The sleep plan

- Make a little star chart where Evie gets rewarded for waiting until morning for her milk. Explain to her, 'You need to rest your tummy when you're in your bed.'
- Give her a toy to cuddle in her bed, as she is used to holding a bottle when she falls asleep.
- After following your usual bedtime routine, give her milk downstairs and then take her to her bedroom. Instead of bringing a bottle in with you, bring a book, her new 'cuddle toy' and a beaker of water.
- Read together, and if Evie asks for milk, explain that she can have some in the morning, but she can't have it at night-time.
- Expect her to protest and be upset, but stay calm and resolute. You know that this is the right thing for her, and that when she drops the feeds, she will benefit in more ways than one. Even though it is tough, she will soon get out of the habit of drinking milk to put herself to sleep.

- Let her know that you are on her side, by reassuring her but not apologizing or trying to appease her. She will feel better about this big change if she can see that you are OK about it and are calm and resolute.
- After reading with her, kiss her good night, tuck her into her bed and leave the room on a very positive note, 'I'm very proud of you, Evie. I'll be back to see you in a few minutes.' Tell her that she must stay in her bed. Leave the room with confidence; do not fully close the door.
- When she has her milk, she usually falls asleep very easily, but now, without it, she is likely to struggle.
- Return to her within a minute or two if she cries/calls you, and praise her if she has stayed in her bed. Leave again, and return to her every few minutes to praise her for lying down nicely, staying in her bed, trying her best.
- While she is awake and struggling, go to her often and offer your encouragement and reassurance. Let her know that that sleep will come soon, and she doesn't have to try.
- Expect it to take far longer than usual for Evie to fall asleep. You need to give her as long as she needs, and you need to keep your confidence. If you give in and offer her just even a tiny bit of milk to help her settle, you will teach her that, in order to sleep, she needs milk, and in order to get the milk, she has to protest long and hard.
- If she gets out of bed, take her back to bed quietly, and be calm, not cross, when you do this. Stay with her for a just a few moments and tell her that she needs to stay in bed.
- It's best not to tell her to 'go to sleep'. It is better to ask her to lie down quietly/get cosy and so on.
- Sleep will inevitably happen even if she struggles – her internal body clock will ensure it. Also, she will start to enjoy her bedtimes again very soon, even without the milk.
- When she wakes during the night or any time before 7 a.m. and asks for milk/calls for you/comes to your room, you need to go to her/take her back to bed immediately.
- Tell her that she can have milk in the morning. It's fine for her to have a drink of water from her beaker if she is thirsty.
- Go in and out of her room again if you need to, as you did earlier. If she doesn't go back to sleep, just get her up any time after 7 a.m.
- A sleep training clock or just a digital clock with a red display, with all but the second digit covered with tape, will give her a clear idea of when it is morning.

- Once you've let her know that it's getting up time, you can warmly welcome her to the day, and you should find some aspect of her sleeping that has been good, and immediately reward her with specific praise: 'You waited until morning for your milk!'
- Even though she didn't do without the milk out of choice, she should still have a sticker on her chart.

The outcome

Evie had a tough first night without the milk, but Amanda stuck with it and in the morning they both enjoyed the giving and receiving of the praise and the sticker. They went 'cold turkey' on dropping the night feeds, and this was so that Amanda could give a consistent response and also have a very quick resolution to the problem.

It took three nights for Evie to get the hang of falling asleep without the milk, and her daytime appetite very quickly picked up. Now she is eating well in the day and enjoying mealtimes with her mum. She is sleeping through the night and has also finished with the night nappies.

Conclusion

Night feeds in young children don't always cause problems with sleep and daytime appetite, but often they do. Although as a parent, it might feel wrong to withhold food when it is requested; sometimes it's the right thing to do. (Just as you may limit the amount of cake and sweets that your child has at a party!)

Although Amanda decided to drop the night feeds all at once, if this feels like too much for you, you can do it gradually. But if you do this, rather than cutting the number of feeds and feeding at one waking but not at another, it is best and less confusing for your child to offer a smaller amount at *every* waking. If you're bottle feeding, you can also dilute the milk, gradually increasing the ratio of water to milk.

If you're dropping night feeds, whether breastfeeds or bottle feeds, a good place to start is by not feeding your child to sleep at the beginning of the night. For bottle-fed children, you can give them a cup or beaker of milk with their bedtime stories, and if you're using a lidded beaker, avoid the spill-proof ones where your child has to suck to get the milk. It is better to use one with a free-flowing mechanism, where they can sip and drink. When the bedtime stories are finished and you've said good night, you should take the milk away or replace it with a drink of water.

After this, follow the principles of the previous case studies, where you alter the bedtime routine to set the scene for change. This will give you the chance of making changes during the night in the light of the bedtime changes.

For breastfed children, you might want to start by giving the final breastfeed in another room and then taking them to the room where they usually sleep in and have a cuddle and a story. If they ask for the breast, tell them that their tummy needs to rest at night and they can have milk in the morning. If they protest or get upset, you can reassure them without feeding them. I know that this can be really tough, as children who are breastfeeding often love to suckle as their primary means of comfort. Once again, a comfort toy for them to hold on to or even to suck or chew on can be helpful – and there is no need for you to leave your child on their own. It's OK to stay and support them.

Most toddlers and young children who are breastfeeding in the night tend on the whole to just have very short feeds – just little sips or 'shots' of milk. If this is the case for your child, then if and when you're ready to stop the night feeds, you are better dropping them all at once. If your child is taking longer feeds (usually from about 4 a.m. onwards), then try instead to gradually cut the duration of these feeds. Be warned, though – your little one may get very *annoyed* if you take them off the breast before they've finished (in other words, gone to sleep!).

Some couples when they are trying to drop their child's night breastfeeds will get the non-breastfeeding parent to put their child to bed and respond to the night wakings. While this might work for many, I'm not sure that it is the best way – for the following reasons:

- The child may feel that the non-breastfeeding parent is taking them away from the breastfeeding parent, and as a result may consider them to be 'the enemy'.

- When the breastfeeding parent eventually starts putting the child to bed again and responding in the night, the child may feel that things are now 'back to normal'. As a result, even though they may have learned how to sleep without the breast, they will have to learn all over again with the returned breastfeeding parent.

- There is something quite important and actually quite lovely about the parent who started the breastfeeding journey being the one to gently draw it to an end. Only when the time is right, of course. I know this from my own experience of breastfeeding my own four children.

Case study
Twenty-month-old toddler, Salvatore, breastfeeding six to eight times at night and not eating well in the day.

The situation
Salvatore was a healthy toddler who was developing well and was happy during the day. His appetite was small, however, and he took most of his nutrition in the night in the form of breast milk. He was not underweight, and he liked food, though he only ate small amounts and had to be distracted in order to do so.

He always started the night in his cot, which was in the main bedroom, and he was always breastfed to sleep at the beginning of the night. Sometimes this could take over half an hour. And if he woke up as he was being put into his cot, he would cry and need feeding again or rocking to sleep. He was getting heavy, and Valeria's back was suffering.

When he woke in the night he moved to his mother's bed and then he slept in there for the night, as this helped her to get some sleep. His father, Tomas, slept in Salvatore's nursery, on a sofa bed. Both parents wanted Salvatore to sleep in his cot and sleep through the night.

The solution
Now that Salvatore was nearly two years old, he did not need to have night feeds anymore from a physiological point of view. This

was the case even if he hadn't eaten a great deal of solid food during the day. Dropping his night breastfeeds did not mean that he had to give up breastfeeding completely. He could still have a bedtime and a morning feed as well as breastfeeds in the day, along with his solid food.

Valeria needed to stop the night breastfeeds and teach Salvatore how to put himself to sleep without the nipple in his mouth. She could do this in a loving and responsive way. Once Salvatore had learned some independent sleep skills, it would mean that Tomas was equally able to put him to bed and respond if he woke in the night.

The sleep plan

- Move Salvatore's cot to his own room. The change in sleep environment will help him to accept the other changes.
- Bath him every night still and then, once he's ready for bed, take him through to his new room and offer him his final breastfeed, sitting in a chair or on floor cushions.
- Keep the curtains open or the light on, so that the room is quite bright. Then cut the duration of the feed so that he doesn't get too sleepy. After the feed you look at a simple baby book together (the same one each night). Then put the book away, turn the light off/ close the curtains, but keep the door ajar and put him into his cot while he is clearly wide awake.
- The change in the routine will make him more wakeful and perhaps even tearful, but put him into his cot regardless. Do not wait for him to appear sleepy.
- As soon as he cries, you should kneel beside him, allow him to stand up or kneel up if he wants to, and then hold him as he is standing/kneeling/sitting and give as much physical contact as he needs (while keeping him in the cot) – you can pat/stroke down his back/comfort him physically.
- Speak softly/sing to him or use a repeated soothing phrase/song that he will come to recognize as a sleep signifier but do not lift him from the cot and do not feed him again.
- Accept his crying for what it is – frustration that you are not following the familiar settling routine of feeding him to sleep.
- Every 2–3 minutes or so, you can lay him down if he will let you, but at first he will get straight back up. When he does this, you should hold him again. Give him time.
- As he eventually becomes calm and allows you to lay him down, withdraw the amount of your contact, until you are sitting beside

his cot and softly patting the mattress. Do stay with him, if you think he needs it, and expect the whole process to take about an hour, though it could be longer – there is no upper time limit.

- Once he is asleep, go to bed as early as you can, and be mentally prepared to be up in the night with him when he wakes up.
- When he wakes, you should go to him quickly if he is calling for you, and then reposition him or let him stand if he wants to, and kneel or sit beside him, holding him and repeating the sleepy phrase as you did earlier. Once again, please do not feed him and try not to get him out of the cot.
- It will be difficult at first – especially during the restless latter part of the night – but you do need to stick with it.
- Treat any time before about 7 a.m. as if it is a night waking. If he sleeps beyond this time, you should wake him when it gets to 8 a.m.
- Before getting him up, open the bedroom blind/curtains and put the light on, to offer him a visual clue that it is now daytime and give him an emphatic 'Good morning!'
- Then bring him into the living room (not your bed, as that might confuse him) and start the day with a breastfeed, cup of milk or breakfast.
- Valeria, you might have to express some of your milk in the night for your own comfort, but your body will soon adjust to making milk for the times that it is needed. As you know, breastfeeding is about supply and demand!

Daytime naps
- When you put him in his cot for the naps, you need to do it after at least one night of the new routine. It is important that for daytime cot naps, he is settled in exactly the same way as at night-time, so go to his room; change his nappy; feed if he's due a feed; share the baby book (the same one as at night-time) and then put him into the cot awake. Sit with him until he eventually goes to sleep.

You don't have use a pre-nap routine if he is just going to sleep in his pram or has a contact nap in your arms.

Tomas putting Salvatore to bed – nights 3 and 4
- Valeria should start this process, and then after two or three nights Tomas can put Salvatore to bed. By then, he'll be used to the new routine and his own self-soothing skills will be more well developed.

- Tomas can stay or come in the bedroom after Salvatore's breast-feed and read the book that Valeria has established; then put Salvatore into his cot awake. He should stay with him if Salvatore cries, responding in the same way that Valeria has done.
- Tomas can then go to him if he wakes in the night, as he will have overcome the expectation of the night breastfeeds, and then Tomas can settle him in the same way as he did at bedtime.

Moving forward – night 5

- Valeria, after following the new routine, with the shorter feed and the book, you need to move on a bit tonight. You do the first night of this new phase, and then Tomas do the next one. After that, you should alternate as much as possible.
- Pop him into the cot after the familiar last story; kiss him good night and then leave the room, but still leave the door semi open.
- Return every 1–2 minutes, very briefly (10 seconds maximum) until he goes to sleep during one of your absences.
- Each time you go in to him, you can reposition him/lay him down if he needs you to. It is fine to speak to him in a loving and reassuring manner. It is also fine to give him a little kiss, but **you should not be waiting with him to settle.** The purpose of you going in is just to reassure that you are close by. He will learn the settling bit by himself. So you need to leave again after a few seconds even if he is still fussing/awake. Don't worry – you'll soon be going back to him!
- It's OK, while you are out of the room, to call to him, 'I'm coming in a minute, Salvatore!'
- Even if it takes a long time for him to settle, you should aim not to be in the room with him as he goes to sleep.
- As he sounds more sleepy, just listen out for him rather than going in.
- What is most important is your manner. You need to be calm, loving and confident – so even though he feels strange about the change, he can see that you are calm and are in control.
- If he wakes in the night, you need to respond in the same way.
- Within a week or so (if you follow the plan completely), he is very likely to be sleeping through the night and he will still be the lovely happy boy that you know.

Outcome

Salvatore struggled to fall asleep at bedtime for the first two nights, but from the very first night there was a reduction in his number of wakings. On the first night he woke twice – for 45 minutes at 11.30 p.m.

and then for 15 minutes at 4 a.m. He then slept through until 6.30 a.m. On the second night he woke at 12.15 a.m. for 10 minutes and then slept through until 4 a.m. After this, he was very restless and in light and broken sleep until Valeria got him up at 6 a.m. At all of these wakings, his mother was there to reassure him and help him resettle in the way that she had taught him to do at the start of the night. Over the coming nights Salvatore settled in his cot at the start of the night without crying and the night wakings gradually became fewer and shorter, as he figured out how to self-settle and join his sleep cycles. There was a renewal of the crying when the family moved on to the next stage when they left the room, but this only lasted for about 20 minutes. After that, his parents heard him wake in the night, but he just chatted a bit and then went back off to sleep. His good sleep habits have continued, with him sleeping through from 6:30 - 7am and he very soon started eating well in the daytime. Valeria continued to breastfeed him until he was two years old, which is what she had always planned to do. When it came to giving up completely, it was easier for both of them that Salvatore's sleep didn't depend upon it.

Conclusion

Because Salvatore's parents were ready for change and were able to understand the reason for his frequent night waking and excessive night feeding, they were able to solve his sleep difficulties in a sensitive and confident way. They liked being able to tackle the problem in two stages and the fact that they could work together. Sleep problems are always more successfully treated if the family is able to accept and understand the reasons for the offered solution.

Early waking

Most young children are naturally early risers, and if your child is full of energy at 6 a.m., after having had ten hours or more of sleep, then this is probably something that you have to accept and go along with.

However, if your child wakes up early and still looks or seems tired, then it is good to help them learn how to sleep for longer. A warning, though: early waking can be much more difficult to tackle than other sleep problems. This is because sleep becomes much lighter as daytime approaches, and when your child has had a long block of sleep (even if it is not enough), they will usually find it a challenge to resettle when they wake after 4 a.m. Of course, keeping the room as dark as possible will help them to realize that it is night-time, and keep their melatonin production going, so it is worth getting a blackout blind or curtains – especially in the summer or if there is significant street lighting outside your child's room. Sleeping in the dark is definitely best for young children, but as I've mentioned before, if they don't like to be in the pitch black, you can use a night light, with a red glow.

Putting them to bed later in the evening rarely makes any difference to the time that they wake in the morning. The main reason for this is that, if they stay up too late, they may become overtired, and when they are overtired at bedtime, they are likely to have higher levels of cortisol. Cortisol is the hormone that keeps us awake and melatonin is the hormone that puts us to sleep. As morning approaches, cortisol levels rise in preparation for the day, and melatonin levels drop. If a child (or adult for that matter) falls asleep with high levels of cortisol on board, there is a high chance that the natural junction where melatonin drops and cortisol rises will happen earlier. If anything, putting your child to bed *earlier* than usual can help them to sleep in later in the morning.

Parents vary in their opinions about what constitutes an acceptable getting-up time, but generally, any time after 6 a.m. can be considered a normal wake-up time for most young children.

Insight: Larks and owls

The terms 'larks' and 'owls' describe a natural 'morning person' and a natural 'evening person'. In technical terms they are known as **chronotypes**. Most (but not all) young children's chronotype is that of the morning lark, meaning that they are at their best earlier in the day. These little larks are natural early risers and need an early bedtime. If you have a night owl, (although this chronotype is more common in teenagers than preschoolers), your child will be at their best later in the day and in the evening. These little owls will struggle to get to sleep at an early bedtime and will find it hard to wake up in the morning. Even if you 'train' their circadian rhythm by waking them early, for day care for example, they will naturally still be at their best and brightest later in the day.

Chronotypes aside, I have found that a lot of early-waking problems are in fact the same as night-time waking problems, except they are happening later in the night. For example, some children who fall asleep with a parent beside them may not actually become aware that their parent is no longer there until about 5 a.m. Or they may have already woken earlier in the night and been able to resettle with a bit of reassurance or a parent sitting beside them again. But when they wake again and it is after 4 a.m., when their levels of sleep hormone are dropping, they will find it much more difficult to return to sleep without their parent beside them, than they did earlier in the night.

Lots of young children miss out on the final sleep cycle of the night because their self-settling skills *at the start of the night* are not strong. It's good for them to practise these skills when they first go to bed, as this is the time when they are naturally most able to sleep. If they become confident and able to sleep alone at this time, then they will be better able to join their sleep cycles even towards morning, when they are naturally becoming more wakeful.

If your child is settling completely independently at bedtime and is sleeping through the night but still waking up very early, you could consider using a technique called scheduled awakening. This is often used to treat night terrors and sleepwalking, but it can also sometimes work with early waking. How it works is that about 15–30 minutes before your child usually wakes for the day, you go in and gently rouse them a little bit without fully waking them up. This disrupts their sleep cycle and causes them to enter a new one.

Sleep training clocks and lamps

These can be really useful for letting a child who is too young to tell the time know when it is time to get up. There are some golden rules to follow when you're using a sleep training clock:

- Choose a clock that has a red or orange glow. Some sleep training clocks have a blue back light, which interferes with melatonin production.
- Set the clock to 'wake up' at a time just a few minutes after your child's natural wake-up time, even if this is very early, and then gradually move the time forward as your child understands the principle of waiting in their bed. If they learn to wait in their bed, they have the opportunity to fall back to sleep. Setting the clock very much later than your child's usual wake up time can be discouraging, and may set them up to fail. It's better to be honest and realistic.
- With a very young child, there is no need to explain the principle of how the clock works. They will learn it by experience.
- *You* must obey the clock if you expect your child to! It's no good setting it for 7 a.m. and then getting your child up before then, while the clock is in sleep mode. If you do this, they will learn that waiting for the clock to wake up is optional.
- Don't let your child play with the clock! In so many cases, children run into their parents' room at ridiculous o'clock, holding the device which is now on day mode, because *they* have altered the wake-up time.

Case study
Two-and-a-half-year-old boy, William, waking at 4.30–5 a.m. every morning.

The problem
William was a healthy boy who usually was a good sleeper, from 7 p.m. to 7 a.m. Recently, he had started waking very early in the

morning. As a result, he was taking a very long morning nap of around three hours, instead of his usual midday nap of an hour and a half.

The family was due to have a new baby in a few weeks' time and William's parents were concerned about how he and they would cope.

The solution

William needed to understand when it was time to get up and when it was time to stay in bed. A sleep training clock would be used to help him, and he would have rewards for waiting in his bed until getting-up time.

He also needed to change his nap times, as the lengthy morning nap was 'enabling' the early waking. It also meant that, after his morning nap, he had too long a stretch until his usual 7 p.m. bedtime, and by the time he was put to bed he was overtired. Overtiredness can cause early waking and he was in a vicious circle.

The sleep plan

- Get a sleep training clock with a red night light, and set it initially for 4.45 a.m.
- Set up a reward system – an empty jam jar and pieces of dried pasta (you decide on the size of each). For staying in his bed until the clock wakes up, he can put a piece of pasta into his jar. When the jar is full, he gets a special treat.
- If William wants to nap in the morning, limit it to about 20 minutes. Then let him have his main nap of one and a half to two hours, just after his lunch.
- Keep going with your usual bedtime. Putting him to bed later will not mean that he wakes later in the morning, and he may end up overtired. If anything, put him to bed a little earlier than usual, so that he has a real sense of falling asleep rather than 'crashing out'.
- Make sure that, when he goes to sleep, he is aware that you have left the room.
- When he wakes any time before 4.45 a.m., keep him in his bed. Stay beside him if you need to, and then when it gets to 4.45, you should remark that the clock has woken up and now it's time for William to get up!
- Warmly welcome him to the day and immediately reward him with specific praise: 'You waited in bed until your clock woke up!' Do this even there have been tears and resistance. Reinforce the praise with a piece of pasta for his jar.

- After two days, move the getting up time to 5 a.m., and then if he is able to wait in bed for the clock, keep moving it forward by 15 minutes every two days until you get to 7 a.m. It will take nearly three weeks, but it is better to do this gradually.
- At first, you will teach him merely to wait in his bed, but then he will eventually learn how to settle back to sleep.
- You need to have confidence with this, as it is absolutely possible for William to learn how to sleep for longer. He just needs you to show him the way!

The outcome

William very quickly figured out what the sleep clock was for, and he enjoyed getting praised for waiting in his bed. His parents were initially impatient to set the clock for 7 a.m. on the first day. It was explained how doing it gradually would be better for William, and he would be less likely lose heart through being given an overly difficult challenge. William, in fact, began sleeping through to 7 a.m. when the clock was still set for 6 a.m. It was lovely for him to wake up to a feeling of success!

The morning nap was soon stopped as it was no longer needed, and William was then able to re-establish the one single nap in the middle of the day.

All this was achieved before the arrival of his baby sister, Amelia.

Conclusion

Early waking can be challenging, as biology, wake hormones and (in the summer) light levels are working against your child. But with very clear behavioural techniques, sensitive timings and encouragement, it is usually possible to help your child wake up later in the morning.

Early waking and daytime naps

As we have discussed, overtiredness can lead to early waking, and so it's great if you can keep the daytime naps going for as long as possible. However, if your child's only nap is early in the morning, then that is a continuation of their night's sleep and it can easily become 'set' with your child's internal clock.

This will lead to the continuation of the early waking, which is now enabled by the early nap. Not only this, but the early nap is likely to make your child's lunch-time nap impossible, meaning that they will either want to sleep too late in the day, or they will be overtired by bedtime.

There are two ways of dealing with this:

- Drop the morning nap completely, and push them on to the lunch-time nap, giving them an earlier lunch for a few days, to help them make it.
- As in the case study, give a very short morning nap, just to break the build-up of their sleep pressure, and then let them have their main nap around lunch time. In this instance, you may give them a slightly *later* lunch to enable them to build up sufficient sleep pressure to be able to sleep again.

Either way, once the early waking has resolved, your child will be able to make it comfortably to the lunch-time nap – before eventually dropping the naps completely and making it to (an earlier) bedtime.

Nightmares

Nightmares or scary dreams are very common indeed in young children, and almost all two- to five-year-olds will have the odd one. Almost a quarter of children in this age group will have recurrent or chronic nightmares. Because nightmares are far more common in children than they are in adults, they can be seen as a normal part of child development.

Nightmares tend to happen later on in the night, when children experience more rapid eye movement sleep (REM sleep). REM sleep is often called 'dream sleep', in fact. During a nightmare a child is very unlikely to move, talk or cry out, but they will often wake and cry *afterwards*. Usually, they can remember what the scary dream was about, and sometimes even long after they have woken up, later in the day, they will still be troubled by it. It's not uncommon for children to be so upset by a nightmare that they are afraid to go to bed at night. As with bedtime fears, a child's nightmares reflect where they at in terms of their development. A child of two is more likely to dream about scary monsters, whereas a child of five is more likely to dream about something upsetting that they've seen in the day – either a real-life event or a film or video.

While a child having a nightmare can be thought of as normal, if they are happening very frequently it is advisable to speak to your child's doctor. The same is true if the dreams are about the same thing each time, or are causing your child to be fearful or anxious in the day.

The main factors which are known to make the nightmares worse or more frequent are:

- not getting enough sleep – when children are overtired, they are more likely to have nightmares;
- stress or trauma – nightmares which follow an upsetting or traumatic incident in your child's life, will usually start about three months after the event;
- family tendency for nightmares – if you or your partner had or have nightmares, there is more potential for your child to have them; too;
- anxiety – If your child is generally anxious and/or has separation anxiety, they may have a greater tendency towards nightmares.

Young children don't find it easy to tell the difference between dreaming and reality, and it is really helpful for them if you emphasize the message that their bad dream was not real life. During the day explain that bad dreams are normal, not real, and they do not come true.

The best ways to help your child with nightmares are:

- Make sure that they have early nights and are well rested.
- Follow a reassuringly repetitive bedtime routine, to help them feel safe.

- Try to end the day on a calm and happy note, so that your child doesn't feel stressed as they are falling asleep.
- Avoid having them watch scary films, and if you know that they are sensitive or anxious, be careful about books with scary content, too.
- If they wake from a nightmare and they are upset, reassure them and explain that it was just a dream.
- Encourage them to them to repeat a simple mantra such as 'It's gone now – silly dream!'
- If your child is old enough, teach them how to change the ending of a bad dream into a funny or safe one – for example, the giant that was chasing them turns into a little mouse and runs away!
- Try always to act in a way that is calm and reassuring. If they are feeling frightened and out of control, they need to know that you are strong and they are safe.
- After you have given them some reassurance, it's better that they go back to sleep in their own bed rather than getting in with you. First, coming into your bed may become a habit, and second, it may give validation to the dream and their fears that actually they are not safe on their own.
- For the same reasons, it is best that you don't sleep on their bedroom floor or in their bed with them.

Insight

It is normal for children to wake in the night. There doesn't need to be a reason. When they wake in the night and call for you, it is better to tell them that it's still night-time, they've woken up too soon, and everything is OK.

If you ask them what is wrong, they may think that something *should* be wrong, or even feel under pressure to think of something! 'I've had a bad dream/I've got tummy ache/my bed feels scratchy!'

Of course, if they tell you any of these things, then you will respond with comfort and reassurance, but let them tell you first without you asking or giving them a list of options.

Problems associated with deep sleep

Night terrors (sleep terrors)

Many people think that a night terror is a very severe nightmare, but in fact it is something quite different. Along with sleepwalking and sleep talking, night terrors are known in sleep science as a disorder of arousal. They happen when there is a *very* slight awakening during deep (NREM) sleep, usually *early in the night* – typically 1–3 hours after the child has gone to sleep.

During a night terror a child will usually thrash around and often cry and call out. They can look terrified (hence the name) and they may also be sweating and have a racing pulse. Although they look like they are awake, they are not, and therefore they will not respond to you trying to comfort and reassure them. The whole event can last for anything between a few minutes to over an hour. Although they are very dramatic and distressing for parents to see, the child doesn't wake up and usually can't remember anything about it in the morning. It is often said that the night terror is worse for the parents than for the child. These episodes can also happen during deep sleep within naps, which is why, technically, they are called sleep, not night, terrors.

It's very important to understand that sleep terrors are connected with brain development and are not usually caused by emotional or psychological issues. Neither does the experience of having a sleep terror *cause* any emotional or psychological damage to a child. However, if your child has a tendency towards having them, they can be worse at stressful times.

Traditionally it has been thought that night terrors start at around the age of four, but a recent study found that they can start from about 18 months old. The same study also found that just over half of all children will experience at least one night terror at some point before the age of 13. Often with a younger child, a confusional arousal (see below) can be mistaken for a night terror, as they occur at the same time of night and have similar features.

Night terrors affect between 1 per cent and 6 per cent of children, so they are not that common, and while they can continue throughout childhood, they are usually worse and more frequent when they first start happening and then gradually improve and are outgrown by adolescence. *However*, children who have experienced night terrors when they are small will often continue with, or go on to become, sleepwalkers or sleep talkers!

Night terrors, sleepwalking and sleep talking often run in families. If you or your partner had or have any of these, there is an increased chance that your child will, too.

Some of the things that make night terrors worse or more frequent are:

- overtiredness (sleep deprivation)
- a high temperature during illness
- separation or general anxiety
- inconsistent sleep routines
- sudden loud noise when your child is in deep sleep.

And, in addition, some longer-term physical conditions can also make night terrors worse or more frequent:

- obstructive sleep apnoea
- night-time asthma
- restless leg syndrome
- gastro intestinal reflux.

Because your child has no recollection of the night terror, there is no point in discussing the episode with them afterwards, as you might do if it was a nightmare. However, if you are changing their bedroom around and moving things that out of the way that they could hurt themselves on, it is the right thing to explain the night terrors to them in simple and harmless terms. For example, according to their age, you might say something along the lines of, 'Sometimes when you are deeply asleep, you *stomp, shout and move about* ... and you don't even wake up!' Reassure them that lots of children do the same thing, and that they will grow out of it. Tell them (if it's true) that you or your partner used to do the same when you were children. You should also explain their night terrors to them if you are talking to their siblings about them, or are preparing them to go for a sleep over with family or friends.

Here's what you can do to prevent and manage their sleep terrors:

- Avoid your child becoming sleep deprived and keep a very regular sleep/wake schedule.
- Make sure that any medical conditions, especially those that affect their breathing are being treated and controlled.
- If they are poorly, keep their temperature controlled with paracetamol, a cool room and clothing, and plenty of fluids
- Have a consistent bedtime routine and do the best that you can to create a calm atmosphere in your home, especially before bedtime.
- Keep your child's sleep space safe and remove any pieces of furniture that they could fall over or hurt themselves on.
- Have a dim, red night light on, so that you can see them and keep them safe if they experience a night terror.
- During an episode **do not try to wake your child.** It will not help, and it could cause them to feel distressed if they wake up and don't recognize you at first.
- Stay calm, stay quiet, stay with them and keep them safe.
- Be patient, don't panic – just wait for the episode to pass.
- When it is over, guide them back to bed if they've got out and let them continue to sleep.

If your child's night terror happens at the same time either every night or on the nights where they have one, you can try something called 'scheduled awakening'.

Scheduled awakening is a technique that can be used to treat night terrors and sleepwalking. About 15–30 minutes before you predict that your child is going to experience an episode, you go them and semi-wake them up. The best way to do this is by repositioning them, tucking them in, and telling them that you love them. This disrupts their sleep cycle and causes them to enter a new one, often 'bypassing' the night terror. Don't wake them up fully as this may upset and confuse them. Equally, don't be too tentative as you may not rouse them enough, and the technique won't work. They need to come into lighter sleep but still have their eyes closed.

Note: Scheduled awakening can also be used to try to extend the night of a child who wakes up too early in the morning.

Confusional arousals

These are very common in toddlers and young children, and they can easily be mistaken for night terrors. In fact, in very young children, **confusional arousals are far more common than night terrors**, and around 17 per cent of young children will experience them. They mainly happen early in the night if a child stirs or is awoken during non REM sleep (deep) sleep. Sometimes these episodes can happen when they are waking up first thing in the morning as well. Typically, they will be sitting up in their cot or bed, with their eyes open and crying things like 'No! No! No!' Sometimes they will be just moaning or whimpering. They are still asleep, and so they will seem disoriented and in another world. They will be difficult to rouse, and this is one of the ways that helps you to distinguish a confusional arousal from a nightmare. Often, they will seem angry and will fight you off if you try to comfort them. Confusional arousals usually last for about 5–15 minutes. As with night terrors, children don't tend to remember the event, and it is not a sign of emotional or psychological difficulties, but rather a developmental stage that lots of children go through and eventually grow out of.

As with night terrors, to prevent these confusional arousals from happening, you need to avoid letting your child become overtired, and when they are unwell, pay attention to keeping their temperature down. If the arousals are happening most nights and at the same time, you can try the scheduled awakening technique, mentioned earlier. When your child is experiencing an episode, it is best to sit quietly beside them and let it run its course rather than trying to wake them up.

Another really helpful thing that you can do to help is to make sure that when your child goes to sleep, they are in the same conditions as they will find themselves in when they naturally wake in their sleep later on. If they fall asleep with the light on/ you sitting next to them/music playing and so on, and then they wake later and the light is off/you're gone/the music has stopped, they will understandably feel strange and upset.

Sleepwalking

Sleepwalking is very like a confusional arousal except the child gets out of bed and walks around. About one in five young children sleepwalk at some point, and they usually grow out of it by the time that they get into their teens, although a few will carry on into young adulthood.

As with the other disorders of arousal, namely night terrors and confusional arousals, sleepwalking happens during very deep non REM sleep, usually at the start of the night. When it happens, you might think that your child has intentionally got up and come to find you, but then you realize that, even though they are walking around with their eyes open, they are in fact still asleep. If you speak to them, they may respond with a bizarre-sounding or nonsensical answer. Sometimes, they may do odd things like taking things out of a cupboard or doing a wee in a waste bin or wardrobe. They are also very clumsy when they sleepwalk and are likely to bump into things or fall downstairs.

Sleepwalking is not usually an emotional thing or a sign that something is wrong with your child. The most concerning thing about it is that potentially a child could walk themselves into a dangerous situation, like falling downstairs, going outside or onto a balcony and so on.

If you have a child that has a tendency to sleepwalk, you need to follow the advice given for the prevention and treatment of *all* the confusional arousals:

- Don't let them get overtired.
- Have a familiar and repetitive bedtime routine.
- Keep their temperature controlled when they are unwell.
- Don't wake them during an episode, but stay with them to make sure that they are safe.
- Try scheduled awakening if they repeatedly sleepwalk at the same time each night.
- Have a dim red night light on so they can see where they are going if they get up, and you can see them.
- And, in addition to the above, if your child is a sleepwalker:
  - Have a stair gate in their bedroom doorway or at the top of the stairs.
  - Don't give them the top bunk!
  - Keep all windows and doors locked at night.
  - Keep their sleep space tidy, and don't leave toys out on the floor that they could tread on and hurt themselves.
  - If they are going on a sleepover, explain to the adult looking after them what they need to do to keep your child safe.
  - Sleepwalking often happens when a child is in a different place. So when you go on holiday, keep a special eye on them and lock any balcony doors and keep them safely inside the tent or caravan and so on.

Insight: The difference between nightmares and night terrors

Nightmares are frightening dreams which happen during REM sleep (usually in the last third of the night). A child wakes up and remembers.

Night terrors happen during NREM sleep (usually in the first part of the night). They can be very dramatic and distressing to witness but the child doesn't wake up and doesn't remember.

5

Naps

As adult human beings, we are naturally predisposed, under the influence of our internal body clock, to sleep at night-time and be wakeful in the day. Young children are also naturally inclined to sleep mainly at night, but because they are young and growing, they need to have some daytime sleep, too.

We have already looked at how the period that we are able to remain awake for is influenced by age. Young babies need to sleep every hour or so; school-aged children are usually OK with an awake window of 12–14 hours, and most healthy adults can happily remain awake for 16 hours or more.

There are no hard-and-fast rules about the age at which a child should stop napping. As with all things developmental, every child is different, and whether a child naps or not is often determined not only by their natural make-up but also by external things such as day-care arrangements, cultural factors or even what country they live in. (Children in the USA tend to keep the naps going for longer than children in the UK do!)

That said, the majority of children tend to drop their naps between the ages of three and five, but many will drop the nap before the age of three. The jury is out as to whether having a nap over the age of about three and a half helps or hinders night-time sleep. There is research that supports both sides. In my view, I think it depends upon the child, your lifestyle and also on the timing of the nap.

If your child loves their nap and then settles well at a bed-time that works well for everyone, then there is no need to think about dropping it. In fact, unless your child's nap is causing bedtime problems, it is good to keep it going for as long as possible.

There are some good reasons for this:

- Having a break in the middle of the day will refresh them and they'll enjoy their afternoon more.
- During nap time they experience valuable REM sleep (dream sleep) which we know helps with memory consolidation and learning.
- Research has shown that a midday nap also supports emotional processing, which is so important in this age group, when their feelings can be overwhelming.
- Being well rested through having a nap in the day can actually improve night-time sleep in some children, as sleep helps to keep their cortisol and adrenaline levels low. You may have heard the adage 'Sleep begets sleep!'
- They are more likely to eat well and enjoy running around if they have had a nap and are not tired.
- Having a planned midday nap will help to avoid 'the disastrous 4 p.m. nap' (see below).
- The ideal time for napping is somewhere between noon and 2 p.m. and the ideal duration is 1–2 hours. Any longer than that and your child is likely to feel groggy, out of sorts and take a long time to fully come around when they wake up. Not only that, but you then run the risk of them not being tired enough to sleep when it comes to their bedtime – that is presuming that you want or need their bedtime to be around 7–8 p.m.

How to keep the naps going

As with all aspects of child sleep, consistency is key here. If you have a nap time ritual which is similar to the one that you have at bedtime, you are more likely to keep the nap going for longer.

We know already how behavioural cues can override biological factors when it comes to helping a child to go to sleep, and a fantastic example of that is when a child doesn't nap at home and yet continues to nap when they are at nursery. Simply put, the structured routine in the nursery setting, along with the example of the other children and the direction of the caregivers means that even a toddler who isn't tired will often still manage to have a nap. (If your child is wanting to nap neither at nursery nor at home, then you might have to accept that they have grown out of the need for a regular nap.)

When you put your child down for a nap at home, here are some tips:

- Put them to bed after lunch or a substantial snack, so they are not hungry.
- Follow a routine similar to the bedtime one, with the room darkened.
- There is no need to put pyjamas on, but do put them to bed in light, non-restrictive clothing. Shoes off, of course! If they sleep in a sleep bag, put that on. If not, tuck them under the covers, just as you do at night-time.
- If they don't want to sleep, tell them that they can just have a rest, or some quiet time. Give them some books to look at or put on a recorded story for them to listen to.
- Then if they do go to sleep, they can wake to a tiny gift from 'the nap fairy' (aka you!). A new crayon/a few raisins are all that is needed.
- When they have napped in the day, it's good to take note of what time they settle at bedtime, and then, rather than have a time that is set in stone, set their bedtime according to the appropriate awake window for them. For most children in this age group, that window will be about five hours, give or take an hour each way. So if your child wakes at 2.30 p.m. from the nap, you would normally expect them to settle for the night at about 7.30 p.m.

- If they have missed the nap, then rather than keep bedtime consistently at 7.30 p.m., you should bring it right forward, to as early as 6.30 p.m. This is so that they don't become overtired. Overtiredness at bedtime, as we have seen already, often causes sleep disturbance and early waking.
- If you find that when they have napped, they then can't settle until after 9 p.m. (and you need them to sleep earlier than this), then you may need to restrict the nap or drop it all together. Once the nap has been dropped, your child will then have an 11- to 12-hour awake window, and during young childhood you should try to ensure that they don't stay awake for longer than this. If they wake at 7.30 a.m., their bedtime should be any time between 6.30 p.m. and 7.30 p.m.

The disastrous 4 p.m. nap

Most children go through a stage when they are starting to outgrow the need for a lunchtime nap, but then have an unplanned nap at about 4 p.m. or after.

It is a natural part of the circadian rhythm that we have an energy dip at around 4 p.m. in the afternoon. This is definitely the case for young children, too, especially when they have previously been used to having a midday nap.

Murphy's law would have it that at around 4 p.m. is often when your child is in the car or pram on the school run either for themselves or to collect older siblings. It's also the time where, if your child has been out for the day, they're coming back for tea time. Travelling often lulls a younger child to sleep, and this is not the best time for sleep to happen.

I remember it well with my own children, desperately trying to keep them awake in the car by opening the windows, putting on loud music and even giving them ice lollies, on the way home from a busy day out. (I've just reminded my husband about this, and he says that *he* used to let them sleep because he wanted a bit of peace!)

Actually, unhelpful partners aside, giving a snack at this time can boost their blood sugar a bit and keep them going. If you're collecting your child from school or nursery and driving them home, you might want to take some fruit or crackers with you.

It makes sense to avoid going out in the car or pram at this time unless it is really necessary. If you're able to walk to and from school, and your child is still at the age where they have a pushchair, then encourage them to partly ride and partly walk. Even if this make the journey longer, it is better for their sleep: they'll benefit from the fresh air and exercise, and they will also work up an appetite for their dinner.

If they do end up falling asleep around 4 p.m., then wake them as soon as you can (you might have to cuddle them awake). Then, if they've only had a few minutes of sleep, they may be able to go to bed around their usual bedtime or just slightly later.

How to manage naps in day care and at home

Timing

Often, nap times at nursery or with the childminder are different from the times that you have at home. I usually reassure parents that, as long as the difference isn't huge, there is no need to worry, and it is OK for most children if they have different nap times on the days when they are at home, from the days when they are in day care. However, if your child struggles with this inconsistency, then at home you might find it helpful to adopt the same nap times that your child has in day care.

Although, with younger babies, day nurseries tend to offer a high degree of flexibility, it can be more tricky when they move on to the toddler room or the preschooler room. Here, nap time tends to be more structured and typically is scheduled for just after an early lunch. Lights are turned down, the little sleep mats, pillows and blankets come out, and everyone settles down for sleep. Nursery workers will generally encourage children to sleep for as long as they need to, unless you have asked them to wake your child after a certain time. Outside of the official nap time, children can usually take themselves off or request to have a nap when they need to, but when there are lots of lovely activities and distractions going on around them, they may struggle to settle.

Also, if your child needs help to fall asleep when they are in day care, it might not always be possible for a nursery worker or childminder, who is looking after other children too, to take time out to sit in the 'cosy corner' with yours.

So for these reasons, even if your child is only in day care for a couple of days a week, if they *are* struggling with nap time inconsistency, then it's often more sensible to go with the nursery schedule when they are at home.

Length of the naps in day care

Just as with the timings, the length of naps can often vary between home and a formal day-care setting, and it really can work both ways!

Some children sleep less when they are in a setting with other children, as there is so much going on and it might not be as quiet or as dark as it is when they take their nap at home. On the other hand, there are those who sleep far more when they are away from home and see the other children going off to sleep.

Often, those who have shorter naps in the week when they're away from home will have a long 'catch up' nap at some point over the weekend. This big weekend nap can be really helpful in terms of repaying any sleep deficit, but you may find that, on those big nap days, your child will need a later bedtime. Similarly, if you find that your child has a shorter nap than usual when they are in nursery or with a nanny or childminder, then on those particular days they are very likely to need an earlier bedtime.

As I mentioned earlier, it is the *sequence* of the bedtime routine that is more important than the exact time at which it is done, but it is important that they haven't napped for so long that they won't be able to go to sleep at a reasonable time. This is especially important if they have to be up in time for day care on the following morning!

How they fall asleep when they are not with you

The most important thing when your child is in day care is that they fall asleep happily! And if that means that, when they are with a childminder, family member or at nursery, they get cuddled to sleep, it doesn't matter.

You might have worked very hard to teach them how to settle independently for their night-time sleep and nap times when they are home, and are worried now that others may set things back for your child by overhelping them to go to sleep. The fact is that, because they are in a different setting, and it is a different person to their parent who is settling them, it will not affect what they expect when they are at home.

It is far more important that they are happy when they are away from you, and I'm sure that you want that peace of mind, too. By all means let your child's carer know how they usually settle when they are at home, but also let them know that it's OK for them to give more help if your child needs it.

If your child has a dummy or a comforter, a special toy or a special blanket, make sure that they take these things with them. As I mentioned before, these comfort objects are a very healthy way for children to eventually move towards secure independence.

How and when to eventually drop the naps

To a great extent, you need to follow your child's lead here. Somewhere between about two-and-a-half and three-and-a-half years old, you might notice that the naps are becoming a bit hit and miss – even if you've been following the previously mentioned advice to keep the naps going for as long as possible. There does come a time, though, when pushing the nap thing too hard can potentially end up making them dread their bed, and if they are making it through a nap-free day without getting upset or irritable, then they are growing up and are naturally ready to drop their regular nap.

It is still good to offer them the opportunity to nap if they want to, as, on the odd day, they actually might *want* to have a catch-up nap. (Don't we all!) Don't worry that, if your child starts to want to nap again, that you dropped the nap too soon. As with all nap transitions, the change doesn't happen over-night. (Remember going from three naps to two, then two naps to one?) There is often a period when some days your child will want to nap and others when they definitely *don't* want to.

It is good to respect that, but even if they don't want to nap, do at least give them the opportunity for some quiet time, ideally after lunch, when they can snuggle on the sofa and look at books or even watch a bit of very gentle TV.

When the nap has been consistently dropped, then you will need to bring their bedtime forward, and if they have had settling problems before, they should start to find it easier to fall asleep at bedtime now.

6

Tricky little challenges

Moving your child from a cot to a bed

There is no set time that is right to move a child from their cot to a bed. Often, the decision is prompted by them climbing out, or you needing the cot for a new baby; but more often than not, it is simply the feeling that they are growing up and ready to move on a stage.

Most children move out of the cot and into a bed somewhere between the ages of two and three and a half, but if they are happy in the cot and it is big enough for them, there is no rush or reason to move them at all.

If you are moving your toddler out of the cot to make room for a new baby, it is best to leave a few weeks between moving your older one out and the younger one in. Explain to your child that they are going to sleep in a big bed and let them help you move the cot from the room and put the new bed up. Or, if they are in a cot bed, let them be involved in converting it to a toddler bed.

During the daytime before they actually sleep in the new bed themselves, encourage a game where they tuck their toys into the new bed and then leave them to go to sleep. Praise the toys for going to sleep. Through this small ritual they will receive the subtle message that you will be happy if they do the same.

If they usually wear a sleep bag, now could be a good time to replace it with a little duvet, or sheet and blanket. Similarly, if they still have their milk from a bottle of milk at bedtime, now is a good opportunity to give them a cup instead. If you're giving them a lidded cup, it's best to make sure that it has a free-flowing design rather than being spill-proof. This is so that they learn to sip rather than suck.

Your child can also now have a small flat pillow if you like, although from a physiological point of view they don't really need one. If there are any other changes that you'd like to make, such as getting rid of their dummy or their white noise device, this can be good opportunity to introduce those changes. The reason for this is that often a change in environment can help with a behaviour change or a change in routine.

It is best to avoid keeping the old cot in their room if you can, as this can often cause confusion and night-time bed swapping. Keeping everything as simple as possible and avoiding too many choices at night-time can help a child sleep better.

On the evening of the new bed change, keep up your usual, reassuring bedtime routine before saying good night to them just as you normally do. Don't *expect* any changes, and if you can demonstrate by your manner that all is as normal, your child is more likely to feel OK about the new bed.

Leave the room on a very positive note, even if your child seems a bit unsure, overexcited or very wakeful. Tell them that you will be back very soon to check that they are cosy. Return to them very shortly afterwards and praise them for being in bed (if they are still in it!). Only stay for a few moments before leaving again: say something like 'I'm going to wash my hands now but I'll be back in a minute.'

If your child gets out of bed and comes to find you, it is very tempting to laugh or hug them, as they will look so cute. But, if you do this, they may keep on doing it to entertain you and get the lovely feedback. Quite understandably, they will then be upset and confused when you are no longer finding it funny.

It is better to show them that you are surprised (not angry) that they are up. Quickly and quietly take them back to bed in silence, but as soon as they are in bed, give them the good feedback and praise them warmly.

Leave again even if they are not happy about it but reassure them that you'll be back. If they won't go back to bed, you can try the Standing Quietly technique that I described in James' case study in Chapter 3 and will discuss again in more detail in Chapter 10. Remain standing quietly in the room with them. Tell them just once to go to bed, and then wait in silence until they move towards the bed (it might take a while!). Don't repeat the instruction, but you can say, 'I'm waiting, my love.' Then, when they show even the slightest signs of going back to bed, praise them warmly to encourage them and let them know that you are proud of them.

Don't nag, bribe or get involved in any procrastination or delaying conversation. If they ask for more stories/cuddles/food, you can respond with, 'We'll do that/see to that/get that/talk about that in the morning.'

It's a good idea for both parents, if possible, to alternate going in and settling/praising a child, so that you can reinforce the message that, even though their bed has changed, the 'sleep rules' are the same.

You can expect it to take longer than normal for your child to go to sleep, and this is natural because children like things to be predictable and familiar. The changes that you are making may make them uneasy and wakeful at first.

If your child really does struggle to stay in bed, and you are worried about them wandering about at night, you could consider fitting a safety gate to their bedroom door. If you introduce it in a positive manner – 'This is your gate, to keep you safe!' – there is no reason for them to feel imprisoned.

You will also need to have some kind of soft lighting to keep them safe if they do wander in the night. Choose one with a red glow which will not limit their sleep hormone (melatonin) production.

If they wake and come to you or call for you during the night, you should help them back into bed as you did at the beginning of the night. Go to them every few minutes if they are upset and keep getting up, but try not to be in the room as they settle off to sleep, as this is very likely to then become a habit.

In the morning, offer them lots of *specific* praise: 'You slept in your lovely bed!' 'You went back to bed when I asked you to!'

Coming out of nappies at night and wetting the bed

Night-time dryness almost always follows daytime dryness, and often there is a considerable period in between before your child will manage to achieve dry beds.

You should only ever look towards helping your child to become dry at night when they are reliably dry during the day. As a rule, most children are daytime toilet trained by the time they are three years old, but many are older.

It is not at all unusual for a four or five-year-old to still be in night-time nappies, and even then, many continue to have the odd accident throughout childhood. In fact, one in ten seven-year-olds still regularly wet their bed. Girls tend to be dry at night sooner than boys, but this isn't always the case.

If your child has a very wet nappy in the morning and is no longer taking a night bottle or drinking a lot in the night, this is a sign that they are not yet producing enough of a special hormone called vasopressin. This hormone reduces urine production at night, and until its action kicks in, and if your child is under five, it means that they are probably not yet ready to come out of their nappy or pull-up. It is *perfectly OK* to give them as long as they need, but if they are over five years old and you are worried, you might find it helpful to have a chat with your GP practice, school nurse or health visitor.

You can help your child to develop healthy bladder control by offering plenty of fluids during the day and then stopping them having a drink from an hour before bedtime and dropping feeds or big drinks during the night.

Once they are confident with using the potty or toilet during the day and have dry or nearly dry nappies fairly consistently in the morning, you can take this as a signal that it is time to start night-time toilet training.

Helping your child to become dry at night is more effective if you keep the whole process as relaxed as possible. Suggest that they might like to have a go at sleeping without a nappy. Make sure that you have a waterproof mattress cover on their bed and encourage them to use the toilet before they go to sleep. Don't make a big deal about it or over pressurize them, however.

Many parents choose to lift their children and put them on the toilet later in the evening, just before they go to bed themselves, when the child is asleep. Nowadays, this isn't considered to be a good idea, as the child doesn't learn about bladder control, and it just teaches them to wee in their sleep. From a sleep point of view, it is not good to disrupt that very special and precious deep sleep that happens at the start of the night, either. On top of this, there is also the risk that rousing a child out of deep sleep can cause distress and confusion.

If your child wets their bed, it is best to remain calm and, if they wake up, quickly change the sheets, encourage them to go to the toilet to see if they have any more wee left and then resettle them to sleep. Let them know it's OK, it's not their fault and you're not cross. If your child manages a dry night, praise them gently but don't overdo it, or they might feel they've let you down if they wet their bed next time. Do not use a reward chart, as night-time dryness, or wetness for that matter, is not something that is entirely within their control. You can, however, praise them for the things that they have done to help themselves achieve dry beds, such as waiting until morning to have a drink or for going to the toilet when you ask them to, and so on.

As with so many milestones, helping your child to become dry at night is more effective if you follow their lead.

Tips for night-time toilet training (once your child is dry during the day)

- Encourage your child to drink enough during the day (6–8 glasses), but not fizzy or caffeine-rich drinks. Restricting daytime fluids can cause the bladder to be less efficient.
- If you are still giving a bedtime bottle, now is the time to drop it. If your child is well hydrated during the day, a big drink at bedtime or during the night (unless they are unwell or it is very hot) is not necessary.
- Do not allow your child to get constipated, as this can affect bladder function.
- Use waterproof, easily changeable protection on the bed to minimize night-time disruption.
- Encourage your child to use the toilet just before bedtime.
- Leave a soft light on and, if the toilet is not easily accessible, have a potty in their room.
- If your child wets the bed and wakes up, praise them for telling you and still take them to the toilet to see if they can do a bit more.
- Praise your child gently but warmly when they manage a dry bed and don't expect this to be every night at first.
- Expect just the occasional dry night at the first few attempts.
- If your child doesn't manage a dry bed after 3–4 weeks of trying, you should give up and try again a few weeks later or when they start to have dryish nappies in the morning.

Starting nursery or school

Most parents' concern about their toddler starting day care or nursery centres mainly around the naps. Look back to Chapter 5 for some advice about day care and napping for little ones.

One thing that you might not have considered, however, is how exhausted your child can become when they start school or nursery, and this is especially the case when they have dropped their nap. It's very common for children to be extremely tired when they first start nursery, preschool or school. They will gradually build up the stamina needed to cope with the structured day, but you can help them by letting them have some quiet time to themselves when they get home and putting them to bed earlier. It can be tempting to rush them into making new friends and having play dates, but really, when they have been surrounded by others all day, afterwards they are likely to want just a bit of quiet time on their own and an early night!

If you're working yourself and your child is attending an after-school club, or being looked after by a childminder or family member, ask them to let your child do a quiet activity. At home, having a calm and structured evening routine will help if they are feeling tired or overwhelmed by their day. At the weekends you may find that, if they've dropped their nap, they want to go back to having one, and if this is the case, you should let them do this, even if this means that they then have a slightly later bedtime.

Going on holiday

It is really wonderful to go on holiday with your little ones – a lovely chance to spend more time together away from the usual home routine. Understandably, though, lots of parents are nervous about going away, in case it disrupts the child's sleep, or causes problems on returning home.

It is OK to be a bit flexible with your sleep routines when you're on holiday. If they want to nap in the day and then stay up with you into the evening, this is absolutely all right. It is not necessary to keep to the exact usual bedtime if this doesn't suit you on holiday. When you do put them to bed for the night, however, try to use some of the familiar sleep triggers which are used at home. These include the same songs that you sing around bedtime, the same good-night storybook, familiar sleep bag and the usual teddy/blanket/comforter. It might not be possible to bath your child every night, but you can still use your same bath-time song as you wash hands, face and bottom, and clean teeth.

Even if they are sleeping very close to you, it is better that you continue to settle your child in their own space rather than in bed with you. Not only will this prevent resistance to going into their own bed when you return home, but will also enable you all to sleep better when you are on holiday, too. Having said that, don't be too strict, as no one feels comfortable with a tired, crying child while they are staying in a hotel, tent, caravan or holiday cottage.

If your child is used to sleeping in a very dark room, this same darkness level can be difficult to achieve on holiday. And increased light can lead to early waking – especially if combined with a possible change in time zone. You can darken the room with a portable blackout blind or by using home-made methods such as taping newspapers or pinning blankets to the window frames.

The journey

Children's sleep can be disrupted by travelling, especially long distances. If your child is like most and tends to be lulled to sleep with motion, they may sleep on and off during any journey. Of course, if you have travelled during the day, this can affect their ability to settle down and sleep at night. Their ability to get off to sleep can then be further affected by the fact that they are in a different environment to home.

There are two possible solutions to this:

- Travel during the night or at your child's usual bedtime and let them sleep through the journey.

- Travel during the day but set off early in the morning. And if your little one has slept a lot on the way, put them to bed much later than usual, and then only when they are showing signs of tiredness. They are far less likely to struggle to settle if you do this, and you will avoid all the negative sleep associations and habits which can occasionally develop in relation to a holiday bed.

Plane journeys

If you are intending to travel by plane or if you are going to a country which has a significant time difference, it is worth planning ahead, so that you can minimize any disruption to your child's sleep.

Check in at the airport as early as you can, and don't be afraid to ask if there are any spare seats. They may give you an extra one, so you have more space for your child plus their toys and equipment. Remember that it is in the airline's own interest that you are comfortable. That way, fewer passengers will be disturbed.

As soon as you can after take-off, offer your child a drink. This will help to ease any ear pressure, as well as keeping them nicely hydrated.

Let them sleep as much as they like on the plane. Don't worry if they don't sleep at their usual times. If you're significantly changing the time zone, all of their usual timings will be going out of the window anyway! The most important thing is to avoid them becoming overtired.

Children are more likely than adults to experience ear pain when the plane is landing. Chewing helps, so give them something that will get their jaws working, like a big piece of bread or chewy sweets. Yawning also helps, and yawning is infectious. If you play a game when you pretend to do big yawns, they are likely to follow you! Encourage them to blow their nose, too, as this can help.

Once you've arrived, if your child is awake, allow time to familiarize them with the new surroundings. Then, when they have had a reasonable amount of time to build up some sleep pressure, you can use all your familiar verbal sleep clues in preparation for bed.

Try to go to bed at the same time as your child and let all of you adjust to the time change together. If you are travelling with your partner, you might like to organize yourselves into shifts to deal with the night or very early morning waking which is so common when you change time zones.

If you have travelled long haul, it typically takes about 3–5 days to adjust to the new time. It is possible that your child will adjust more quickly than you, so, to encourage this, allow them to experience as much daylight as possible, either by being outside or being in a sunny room. This will help to set their body clock to sleep at night.

Coming home

On holiday it is only natural that you relax some of your normal rules. The same goes for your children, too. If they are still napping and the naps have been taken mainly on the go, or if your child has slept in your bed or gone to bed very late, then as soon as you come home it is good to get back into your normal routine. Don't put this off – **it's best to use the first night at home to re-establish the 'home rules'.**

You might not be able to put your routine into practice at the usual time, especially if you're back from a different time zone, but you can at least follow the same series of familiar steps leading up to bedtime. If you're coming back after holidaying in a country with a significant time difference, then, as when you first changed time zones, when you're back home, try to sleep when your child does and adjust together. Then within a few days you will all have adjusted, be nicely rested and enjoying happy holiday memories.

Moving house

With all significant life changes, your child will cope better with them if they can see that you are calm with things, and this is especially true with moving house. Because many children find transition and change difficult, it is always good to explain to them, in an age - appropriate, simple and straightforward way, what is going to happen, and allow them to ask questions and express their feelings.

It is good to approach the conversation in a positive way, saying, for example, 'We are going to live in a new flat and you can bring all of your toys.' However, don't let your positivity pressurize them into feeling that they *should* be excited about the move. It's very tempting to say, 'We're going to move to a new flat – isn't that exciting/won't it be great?' You need to be especially careful with your expressed enthusiasm if the move involves them no longer living with one of their parents, or forming a new home with your new partner and possibly step siblings, too. You may be feeling excited about the move, but your child may be not so sure, and it's good to give them the space to express their misgivings.

Moving house or flat can be a lovely new start, but it is undoubtedly stressful and tiring – for both parents and children alike.

Here are some tips to make life easier:

- Prioritize first of all sorting out the place where your child will be sleeping, so that they have somewhere safe and comfortable for nap time and/or bedtime.
- Take a few objects from their old room, so that they feel a sense of security and familiarity.
- Don't rush them off to bed too early on that first night. It would be a shame if their first experience of the new sleeping environment was lying awake and struggling to sleep. Remember, too, that tiredness can help to override feelings of anxiety or fear.

- Keep as many elements from their usual bedtime routine as possible. If you are accustomed to using verbal sleep prompts such as songs and stories as part of your routine, this should be easy for you as these elements are totally portable.
- If you've got all the beds sorted out and made up on that first night, try to avoid bringing your child into the bed with you, unless you have made a conscious choice to bed-share. If you do this, they may get the message that, in the new home, they sleep with the grown-ups!

Saying goodbye to the dummy

If your child still has a dummy now that they are no longer a baby, the chances are that they are very attached to it, and it means a lot to them. There is no doubt that when they were little, the dummy was a useful comforter and it might have got them through some tough times when they had reflux or colic, for example. As they get older, though, it is not the best thing for them to still have a dummy. It can affect the position of their mouth, their teeth and their bite. If it was just their baby teeth that were affected, it wouldn't be such a big deal, but it can also affect their adult teeth, too. Having a dummy can sometimes also affect and delay their speech development.

When they were a baby, it was you who had the control of when and for how long they had their dummy in for, but now that they are older and can help themselves to it, it is easy for you to lose control, and before you know it, they are walking around with the dummy always in their mouth!

If your toddler or child is one of those who wants to have a dummy as a constant companion, your first step towards getting rid of it would be to limit its use to just naps and night-time sleep. Start a morning ritual whereby you and your child put their dummy in a safe place close to their bed so that they can find it when it is time to sleep again. Don't be surprised if, at times during the day, if they are ever upset, they take themselves off to their bedroom to have a few sucks on their dummy! This is allowed, so long as they don't bring it back into the living room with them.

Once they have got used to not routinely having their dummy with them all the time, you may feel that the dummy situation is now reasonable and manageable. It is there to help them sleep but it is not being overused. Once they fall asleep, the dummy tends to fall out of a child's mouth and so the actual time that they have the dummy in for is actually quite short, and not so very likely to interfere with their dentition as it would if it were being used all day.

Some experts believe that, if you take a much-loved dummy away too early, it can lead to thumb sucking, which long term can be more difficult to stop than dummy use. There are a lot of advantages to waiting until your child is emotionally and cognitively ready to understand about no longer having a dummy, and most children will reach this stage of readiness when they are about three or four years old. By this age they will also have dropped or be dropping their daytime nap, so falling asleep at bedtime, without the help of their dummy, will be a bit easier for them as they'll be extra tired.

Try not to get rid of the dummy when you or they are going through any other major changes, such as starting nursery, moving home, potty training or having a medical procedure.

Similarly, if you are expecting a new baby and thinking about getting rid of your older child's dummy, it is best to do it at least six weeks before the birth. This is just so that they can be completely over any dummy dependence and less likely to experience dummy envy if the new baby has one and they don't. Or you can just relax about it and wait until the new baby has settled into the family and your child is used to the change.

If you've decided to wait until your child is old enough to understand, the process of getting rid of the dummy should begin with a conversation and explanation. You need to give a bit of prior notice so that they can get used to the idea. You might want to say something like, 'When we come back from holiday, we will give your dummies to the dummy fairy and get them swapped for something for you to cuddle!' Then have a little ceremony where you collect all of the dummies and put them in a bag with a note for the dummy fairy (who is actually the tooth fairy's cousin). Leave the bag and note in a quiet place and then check later to find a little teddy or other toy in exchange for the dummies. If you don't like the idea of talking about fairies and prefer to be honest, then this is fine! We have after all been talking earlier about explaining to them that monsters etc. are only pretend. You can still swap the dummies for a comfort toy.

When you first put your child to bed without the dummy, do so at bedtime rather than at nap time (if they're still having one). Remember that, in the evening, they are better placed to fall asleep and they have the advantage of their sleep hormones and their familiar bedtime routine to help them. Be prepared to support and encourage them, even if they usually fall asleep very easily. If they struggle to settle, you can explain to them that sleep will come eventually, and they are doing very well. You can let them listen to a story tape if that helps them, and it is fine to keep popping in to their bedroom to let them know that you're behind them.

In the morning, you can reward them with some warm praise, and if you want to reinforce this praise further, you can use a reward chart or other system of collecting tokens for sleeping without the dummy.

Case study
Four-year-old girl, Charlotte, learning to sleep without her dummy.

The situation
Charlotte was a happy child with advanced speech and language skills. She had had a dummy since she was a baby and she used it only for sleep. Charlotte had a nine-month-old baby brother, Oscar,

and each child had their own room. Oscar also had a dummy for sleep. The family had a good bedtime routine and Charlotte settled to sleep by herself at bedtime and, unless she was unwell, she slept through the night. However, she needed her dummy to sleep. Her parents felt that it was time for her to get rid of it now that she was growing up and before she started losing her baby teeth and growing her adult ones.

The solution
Charlotte's parents were advised to explain in advance that she was soon going to learn how to sleep without her dummy. They were to tell her that when her brother, Oscar, was four years old, he would be giving his up as well. It was decided that a good time to get rid of the dummy was the coming weekend, when the extended family were visiting, and Charlotte's older cousin, Violet, who didn't have a dummy anymore, would be coming, too.

The plan
- Because Charlotte loves books, get hold of a simple story about giving up a dummy. I recommend *The Last Noo-Noo* by Jill Murphy (Walker Books, 2011).
- Have this as her final bedtime book for a few nights before you plan to give the dummy up.
- Explain to Charlotte that when Violet comes at the weekend, she will be able to tell her that she has given her dummy to the dummy fairy.
- The day before the family visit, help her to collect all her dummies and put them in a bag. Check everywhere for dummies ... in Mummy's and Daddy's pockets! In the bottom of shopping bags! In the Lego tin! In the sock drawer! ...
- After tea, put the bag of dummies on the window sill and then start your bedtime routine.
- When Charlotte has had her bath, ask her to go to the window sill and see if the dummy fairy has been.
- Let her find a soft, cuddly teddy or animal that she can have to help her go to sleep.
- Once in her room, you can sit together and she can cuddle her new toy as you read your bedtime books – finishing with *The Last Noo-Noo*.
- After this, kiss her good night and leave the room on a very positive note, 'I'm going to come back to see how you're getting on in a

few minutes.' Leave the room with confidence and go out of her line of vision. Have the door slightly open.

- Return to her within a minute or two, whether she cries/calls you or not, and praise her warmly if she has stayed in her bed.
- Leave again, and return to her every few minutes until she is asleep.
- If she struggles to sleep, you can reassure her that sleep will come, ask her to cuddle her toy and let her listen to a calm story tape on a very low volume.
- It is important that, once you've made the decision to get rid of the dummy, you stick with it. It will help Charlotte if you listen to her feelings and are reassuring, calm and resolved about the dummy going.
- If she wakes during the night – no matter how many times before her usual start of 6.30 a.m. – and calls for you, you need to go to her or take her back to bed, and reassure her that she will soon be fine without her dummy.
- In the morning you can warmly welcome her to the day and tell her how well she has done to sleep without her dummy!
- Let her tell the family about her achievement when they come to visit on the following day.

The outcome

Unsurprisingly, Charlotte very quickly learned to sleep happily without her dummy. She felt proud of her success and even told her little brother, Oscar, that when he was a big boy he would swap his dummy for a teddy from the dummy fairy!

Conclusion

If you haven't managed to get rid of the dummy in the first year, it can be tricky to do so in young toddlerhood. Little ones might miss the dummy too much, not understand why it has gone, and sometimes even give up their naps prematurely because of it. There's a strong argument for keeping the dummy and regulating its use – having it just for nap times and bedtime – and then, when they are old enough to reason with and to motivate, get rid of the dummy completely.

Thumb sucking

Babies and toddlers find sucking to be incredibly comforting and soothing. Many like to suck something as they fall asleep, and in the early days, when they are little babies, they often settle by sucking milk from a bottle or breast.

That love of sucking often continues beyond babyhood, and it is common for toddlers to either suck a dummy for comfort when they are not hungry, or suck on their thumb or fingers. It is great when they are able to comfort themselves so effectively, with something so convenient and close to hand. Unlike a dummy or comforter that can get accidentally left behind or lost, your child's thumb is permanently free and available. In the early days this can be brilliant for their sleep, as a child who comforts themselves by sucking their thumb, is often able to fall asleep independently and sleep through the night.

It's a shame to restrict a toddler or young child from sucking their thumb if they like it, and when they are very small, I don't think that there is any need to. You may, however, decide to gently explain to them, when they are old enough to understand, that sucking their thumb is just for sleep time. It is only if the thumb sucking is happening most of the time and continues until they are getting their permanent teeth that you might need to take more definite steps to help them give it up.

By this age it is possible to explain to them that they are getting their big teeth now and they need to look after them very well and help them grow straight. Your dentist will back you up on this and help you reinforce the message. Sometimes, if the advice comes from a person in authority, your child will accept it more readily!

You shouldn't tease your child for sucking their thumb, or tell them that they are a baby. Neither should you tell them off – especially if they are upset, tired and needing their thumb for a bit of comfort. It is better to talk to them about why they need to stop, to gently remind them if they forget, and to encourage them by praising them when they remember.

To help remind them not to suck their thumb, you can put a little novelty sticking plaster on it, and if the plaster stays on all day and doesn't get sucked, they can have a small reward.

I hate the idea of aversion therapy of any kind, but in the spirit of offering choices I have to mention that there is a technique where something nasty tasting, bought from the chemist, can be painted on the child's thumb to discourage them from sucking.

It is true that some children will continue to suck their thumb into older childhood, teens and even beyond, but these people are generally able to regulate their thumb sucking habit, and rarely walk around with their thumbs permanently in their mouths.

7

Family life

A new baby coming into the family

By the time you've got a second, third or more child on the way, there is a good chance that your toddler is established in a stable bedtime routine and is sleeping through the night in their own bed or cot. At least, that's the idea. But if, like thousands of other expectant parents, you are currently bed sharing with your toddler or older child, then it's possible that you might be panicking a bit about how to manage the bed-sharing scenario when the new baby arrives.

If you're not co-sleeping out of choice, and would ideally like your toddler to start sleeping through the night in their own cot or bed, the last thing that you want to do is to 'evict' your precious older one from your bedroom to make room for the little one.

Toddlers and young children come into their parents' bed at night for all kinds of reasons, as we have already seen, and with the extra tiredness that comes with pregnancy it's especially tempting for you to settle them in with you rather than have a battle.

If you've got a big bed and you are bed sharing as a positive choice, then this is absolutely fine – and there is plenty of time later in the pregnancy or further in the future for you to help your child feel happy about staying in their own bed if that's what you want.

If and when you do feel ready, here is a plan of action:

- Be aware that your toddler is likely to need extra reassurance because there is another baby on the way. Talk about it whenever they want to.
- Don't use your pregnancy as a reason to tell them why they need to sleep in their own bed.
- Teach them how to sleep all night in their own bed at least a month before your due date, so they don't feel quite so pushed out by the new baby's arrival.
- If possible, enlist the support of your partner. They are likely to be helping more with your older child when number two, three or more arrives so they need to get into practice anyway!
- Make sure that your toddler learns how to fall asleep in their own bed at the *start* of the night, and never in your bed/on the sofa/somewhere else. As we know, falling asleep in one place and waking up in another can lead to them feeling unsettled, disoriented and needing to find you in the night.
- Have a consistent, reassuring bedtime routine before saying good night to them. After a good-night story, put them into their bed or cot, then leave the room on a very positive note, even if they seem a bit worried. Tell them that you will be back very soon to check that they are cosy.
- Return to them frequently and briefly in a light and reassuring manner: 'I'm going to wash my hands now, but I'll be back in a minute.'
- If they get out of bed, you should stop them at the door and show them that you are surprised that they are up. Quickly and quietly take them back, but as soon as they are in bed, praise them warmly. Leave again even if they are not happy about it, but reassure them that you'll be back.
- If they are in a cot, just go back every couple of minutes to kindly reassure them, lay them back down and leave again.

Don't leave them for long periods alone, and don't be distant or cross when you go back to them.

- Try not to bargain, negotiate or appeal. They can't help the habit they are in, and making them feel guilty about it won't help them to change. At night-time, the whole routine needs to be simple and clear.
- Eventually, they will run out of steam and go to sleep. Don't be in the room with them when this happens.
- When they wake in the night and ask to come into your bed at night, keep them in their own cot or take them back to their own bed straight away. Be calm, not cross when you do this.
- If they keep getting up, you have to keep putting them back – no matter how many times! Remember that this may not be so much an emotional call for help as a reluctance to break a habit.
- Keep your resolve and then in the morning give lots of cuddles and praise: 'You slept in your own bed!'

Your first night is likely to be very disrupted, so you might decide to do this on a weekend when your partner or family is around to support you. If you are resolute, and utterly consistent, you will be successful.

Once you've helped your child to sleep independently, you need to make sure that you maintain this independence, while continuing to reassure them that they are still your beloved and special child.

The following suggestions might help you achieve this:

- A few days before your new baby is due, have the Moses basket/crib/cot ready, next to your bed, so that your toddler is able to understand that that is where their new baby will be sleeping. This way, it will not come as quite such a surprise when the baby comes home.
- When they first see their new baby, whether in the hospital or at home, make sure that your arms are free to hold them.

Allow them to look into the crib in their own time and, as well as giving them the chance to see their new baby, have a special gift in the crib, from the baby, just for them.

- When you first come home, you need to follow your older child's normal routine as much as possible. New-born babies are pretty flexible (certainly more so than toddlers), and if you need to put the little one down for a moment to attend to your older one, the baby will come to no harm, so long as they are placed somewhere safe.

- Always make sure that you continue to put your toddler to bed as usual. You might need to do this with a baby in your arms, but the main focus of attention should be on the older one.

- It is not possible to tell your toddler too much just how much you love them. They really need to hear this when a little one has just come into their life.

- Try not to worry about the new baby crying and waking your older one. Toddlers are surprisingly good at ignoring night-time cries, especially during the first part of the night, when their sleep is deeper. Also, when they hear their baby crying, you will have helped them to understand that it is your responsibility to look after them and not theirs!

Managing bedtime with more than one child

Throughout this book I have referred to child sleep problems in the singular, and you can be forgiven if you are irritated by me not addressing the reality for many, which is that, when you're dealing with a toddler sleep problem, there is very likely to be at least one more child in the family.

I know this very well as at one time in my life, I had four children under the age of six, and bedtimes were not always easy! Having more than one young child to put to bed at night can present simple logistical difficulties: one child needs help with homework, another needs a story, a chat and a cuddle, and yet another needs a nappy change and a feed. Of course, it helps if the children have their own rooms and your partner is home in time to help with bedtime, but for many of us this is not possible. At the end of a tiring day, when everyone's levels of energy and humour are low, bedtime can become a time to dread rather than to enjoy.

If you can find the energy to just give that tiny bit extra at the end of the day for the bedtime routine, it will repay you generously and you will have happy family bedtimes.

I always think that the first thing to do when you want to create *any* kind of event, including a bedtime routine, is to first of all visualize what you want and be really clear about it in your head. Then, when you *know* what you want, you can take the steps to achieve it.

When I work with families, I ask them what they would like their child or family's sleep to be like. It's surprising how many people struggle with voicing it. They may say something like, 'Well ... in an ideal world I wouldn't mind getting up in the night a couple of times and I know that it's too much to expect both of my children to go to bed at the same time of course, but I'd just like things to be a bit less tiring... Sorry if that sounds selfish!'

It is perfectly OK to think and to say, 'I would like to have an easy and harmonious bedtime routine, where I can manage to put my children to bed on my own without help when necessary. I would like them all to go to bed at the same time and sleep through until morning.'

Once your youngest child is about six months old, that is *not* an unreasonable expectation, and what's more, it is achievable. First of all, you need to establish a bedtime routine that is both consistent and meets your children's individual needs. From the age of six months, if not before, your baby can be bathed together in the same bath water with their older sibling(s). It is perfectly all right to run a bath for your toddler, and while supervising them in the bath, you can 'dip' your little one into the water for their bath, too. You can then put the baby into a new nappy and nightclothes, on a clean towel on the floor, while you chat to and watch your older child in the bath. By this age there is no need to have a separate baby bath or bath time for your little one.

(If your children wee in the bath, don't panic. Urine is sterile, which means that it has no germs in it and it will do nobody any harm. If someone poos in the bath, keep calm and get them out of the water. You can then shower or wash them with fresh water and a flannel or a wipe.)

After this, you can go to your bedroom or, if your older child has a room of their own, to their room. While feeding your baby, you can read to or chat with your older one. Then when your baby is fed but still awake, you should encourage a 'kiss good night' ritual and then take your baby to their cot. If this is in their own room, you can ask your older child to wait in bed for you to come back for your final kiss good night and cuddle.

Following the advice given in the original *Gentle Sleep Solutions*, you can settle your baby to sleep in a way that is appropriate for their age and then return to your older one(s) for a final good night kiss and tuck in.

Insight

It is really important that your older child has some exclusive, loving time with you, however brief that might be. It can be hard for them to accept that you are giving the attention that was previously all theirs to another baby. Try to make the time just before sleep for a period of reassurance and special closeness. It will feel really lovely for both of you and will help your child to fall asleep feeling happy.

Sharing a room together

I am a great believer in the advantages of siblings sharing a room together. Children often settle better and feel more secure at night in the close company of a sibling. Another lovely thing about siblings sharing a room is that they have a chance to develop their relationship in a natural way, in the absence of the interference of their parents. They learn about sharing space, respecting privacy and belongings, and about sharing secrets, too. Often, because of limited space, there is no other option than for children to share with one another. If this is the case, they are the lucky ones. Sharing a bedroom is a great preparation for nursery and school and, of course, for later life.

There are, of course, some drawbacks, too, the most obvious one being that, if one child is a poor sleeper, there is a risk that they might wake the other one up during the night or early morning. This is especially common in babyhood and, in particular, with twins, or with older babies and children when they are unwell. Later on, with toddlers and young children, there is the issue of being overexcited after bath time and being too giddy and playful to settle down. Older children who share a room will inevitably experience conflicts over space and personal possessions from time to time.

Case study
Sixteen-month-old Mana and three-and-a-half year-old Anita are sisters learning to share a room together.

The situation
Mana had recently learned how to drop her night feeds and to sleep through the night. She was currently sleeping in a cot in the same room as her parents, and it was felt that the time had come for her to share a room with her big sister. Anita was still in a cot but was ready now to move to a toddler bed. She was excited about having a big bed, her sister moving in with her, and she welcomed the idea of sharing.

Mana was beginning to transition from having two naps to just one. This process was a bit hit and miss. Sometimes she would sleep in the morning, not have an afternoon nap and then be ready to sleep at 5 p.m. This meant that by 7 p.m. she was either inconsolably tired, or if she'd been allowed to nap at 5 p.m., she was still running around at 9 p.m. We needed to make sure that Mana was ready to sleep at the same time as her sister.

The sleep plan

- Drop Mana's morning nap or limit it to 20 minutes. Her main nap in the middle of the day, needs to end by 3 p.m., so that she is ready to sleep at 7 p.m., the same time as her sister.
- Two or three days before the girls are due to move in together, put Anita into her new bed and let her get used to it.
- On the day of moving in together, explain to Anita that today is the day that she and Mana are going to be going to be sleeping in the same room!
- Ask her how she feels about it and listen to her when she tells you. We think that she's excited about the prospect, and it's good to let her share her happy feelings. Listen out for any misgivings, too. Reassure her that, if Mana cries, you will come and take care of her.
- Have a little light-hearted ceremony of moving Mana's cot into the girls' bedroom. Let them role-play getting/being put into bed and going to sleep. Do some clapping and praising!
- Half an hour before bedtime, bathe them together as usual.
- When they're all dressed and ready for bed, sit together on floor cushions in the room or on Anita's bed, and have milk and stories. Both girls should have cups of milk now, rather than bottles. Use lidded beakers if you wish, but make sure that the teats are free-flowing.
- Their final book should be the same each night until they're used to the change. Choose a very simple one that both of them can enjoy.
- Then encourage the girls to kiss one another and you good night and put them both into their cot and bed. Tell them that you are coming back soon to check that they are cosy. Say good night, leave the room and do not fully close the door.
- Return every few minutes if they are awake and chatting. Be kind, confident and reassuring as you tuck them in, give them a little kiss, and so on. Repeat a simple 'sleepy phrase' to each and then leave again.

- If Mana cries, you should stay in the room and reassure Anita that Mana is tired and cross but will soon be asleep.
- Any time that either girl wakes in the night, you should go and reassure/reposition as necessary, then either stay in the room if you think it merits it, or exit and return as you did at the start of the night – using the same calming phrases.
- Avoid 'musical beds'. Each girl needs to stay in her own cot or bed, even if one of them is wakeful and noisy.
- Do not let them get up before 7 a.m. If one or both are awake before this, you need to keep them in bed. If there is just a bit of low-level complaining, chatting or grumbling, you can leave them to it, but if the crying is severe, then you can stay in the room with them until getting-up time.
- When you get them up for the day, open the curtains first, as a daytime signifier. Then give them both a warm welcome to the day and lots of praise for both of them and especially to Anita for being patient and kind.

The outcome

On the first night Mana and Anita were very excited, but they were both tired and fell asleep quickly without having a parent in the room with them. Mana woke very early in the morning, however, and this woke Anita up. One of the parents stayed in the room with them until 7 a.m. and at this time opened the curtains and got them up for the day. Over the coming nights, as the novelty wore off, both girls began to sleep in until close to 7 a.m.

The girls' parents also loved having their bedroom to themselves again and felt that it really improved their own relationship.

Conclusion

It is both convenient and also lovely for siblings to share a room together, and, with some planning and preparation, it is quite a simple process. It helps if you can manage the younger one's naps so that they are ready to sleep at the same time as their older sibling. If Mana had been six months old instead of 16 months old, she would have needed to be awake from about 4.30 or 5 p.m. to be ready to settle back to sleep at 7 p.m. with her sister.

Bringing up your children alone

Whether, at the outset, you made a positive decision to have a child on your own, or whether you find yourself parenting on your own because you and your partner have broken up, bringing up your child or children by yourself has its plus points, at least as far as sleep is concerned. The main advantage is that you are able to focus more fully on your child's and your own needs and are free from the concern of caring for another adult.

Bed and room sharing with your child is less likely to be problematic, as is choosing to go to bed at the same time as your child when you're tired. In two-parent families there can sometimes be disagreements about what time the children should go to bed, whether they should have a bath, and so on. When it's just you, then there is just one way – your way. There are times, of course, when making decisions on your own can feel scary or lonely, and *everyone*, single parent or not, needs to have a support network. For most people, the first port of call is family or friends who have experience with children. In the UK your GP service and health visitor are able to advise you about things relating to your child's health and development. In other countries, your family physician would be a good starting point. And, of course, there is so much support available through online parenting forums. I know that online advice can be conflicting and sometimes misleading, but the main parenting sites are well regulated and have articles written by experts as well as real parents sharing their experiences.

When you have the responsibility of bringing up one or more children on your own, your friends and your family are very important. You should not be afraid to ask for help when you need it. Caring for a child day in and day out is completely demanding, however much you love them. It is hard enough bringing up a child or children when there are two of you, so doing it your own is really admirable. If you are in paid work in addition to looking after your child or children, you will know only too well how little time you have to yourself.

Sometimes parents feel guilty about asking close family and friends for too much practical support like babysitting. If you can afford to buy in some help, then that is great, but for many people this isn't possible. To keep your head above water and get some guilt-free help, it's a really good idea to form a babysitting/child-care group with a small number of trusted friends who would also value some outside help. Take it in turns to look after another friend's child along with your own for the afternoon, and then, in exchange, you can have a free afternoon off yourself. As your child gets older, you may also be able to organize sleepovers, so that you can have an occasional night out.

If you're bringing your child up on your own because you have broken up with your partner, then you will have your own feelings to deal with. You might feel sad, betrayed, disappointed, angry or scared, and on top of these emotions, you have your child's feelings to deal with, as well as their practical and physical care. Often, the best chance that you and your child really have the time to connect is at bedtime, when the busyness of the day is over. This is a really good time to listen to your child's feelings about the family situation and the non-present parent, if they are old enough to express them. It is important to listen and to reassure them that they are safe with you and that your break-up had nothing to do with them. They need to know that they are still loved by both of you. Even if you feel that your partner has behaved badly and you are hurt, it's important to try to hold back from expressing those feelings to your child. They may be the closest person to you, but your negative feelings about your partner need to expressed to another adult rather than to them.

Negotiating sleepovers with your ex

If you and your partner have different viewpoints about managing your child's sleep needs, then sleepovers with the non-resident parent can be really very tricky to handle. In an ideal world, you and your ex would work together to make sure that your child has exactly the same routine and bedtime at both homes. This consistency is so important for them to maintain a healthy sleep pattern, as well as for all of the feelings of security and safety that familiarity brings.

Following the routine that has been established at the more familiar home demonstrates to your child that the parent in the new home is respectful of how things operate when they are not there. By association that also shows respect to the other parent – especially if they were the one who developed the routine. Sometimes the routine and bedtimes need to differ in each parent's home because of other commitments. One father I know has to give his young daughters an earlier-than-usual bedtime when they stay with him on a Sunday night or in the week, as they need to be up earlier in the morning, so that he can take them to day care and get off to work.

Quite often, however, the opposite happens and the parent who has moved out will want to make the time that their child spends with them extra happy and fun, especially at the weekend. Routines can go out of the window, and children are allowed to stay up late, have snacks, watch TV, and so on. All of this is very well intentioned and completely understandable, but it can be very disruptive to a child's sleep, as well as being undermining to the parent who has to deal with the fallout and who is made to feel as though they are the grumpy one!

The very worst thing for your child is to have these visits to their absent parent curtailed, as contact with that parent needs to be encouraged if they are to stay close in the future. If you and your ex-partner are on good terms, then having a calm discussion about your child's sleep needs and reaching an agreement may be all that it needs. If things are difficult between you, and you are having any kind of mediation or couples counselling, then the issue of sleepovers and the importance of how they are managed should be discussed as a priority. If you are not speaking, and not receiving formal help, then maybe a mutual friend or family member, who loves and respects you both, could step in and help.

If your partner is not able to agree to sticking to the usual bedtime routine, and there are no safeguarding issues, then the chaotic sleepovers are something that you may have to accept and work with, rather than trying to stop them happening or letting your child sense your resentment.

Here are some dignified ways to manage sleepovers with your ex:

- Send your child with a nicely packed overnight bag, to show that this is a welcomed event.
- Put a note in it for your ex-partner if there is anything that they should know – such as if your child needs medicine or the arrangements for picking them up.
- Don't include issues between the two of you in the note. Keep it child focused. Try to keep the note as brief and as friendly as possible.
- Plan something nice for yourself to do while your child is away. Go out for the evening, meet a friend or find a good film to watch on your own without distraction. Avoid staying in and doing housework/emails, crying or boiling up with resentment.
- If your child's bedtime routine isn't maintained while they are away, it's not ideal but it's not the end of the world either.
- As soon as they come home, go immediately back to the routine that they know.

- Even very young children are able to recognize that the routine at one home is specific to that place.
- If bedtime at your ex's is completely chaotic and your child is at school or nursery age, try, as much as you can, to schedule overnight visits at the weekend or school holidays.
- Try to keep a sense of proportion and honesty. Is the routine at your ex's *really* that bad, or are you just hurt and angry that they are having fun together?
- Remember that, even though your life might be better without your ex, you need to keep the door open to them for your child.

Adopted children

When you've adopted a child, it is so easy to feel daunted by the challenges that come with helping them to grow up feeling loved, happy and emotionally secure. It is very important for you to realize that you are not on your own, and that *all* parents feel the same way. Something which may be unique to your situation, however, is that you might not have had your child from when they were first born and, even if you have, the information about their birth history or family health history might be limited.

In some ways this can work to your advantage, especially if you can have the confidence to know that the most important information you need to help your child to sleep well is right in front of your eyes. Your interpretation of their needs and your response to them is what matters most, and you are every bit as capable of meeting their needs as you would be if you were their birth parent.

If you adopt your child as a toddler or young child, it is helpful to get as much information about their sleep as you can. So ask the foster carer, social worker or their family member the following:

- Do they have a dummy?
- Do they have a night bottle?
- Do they have a comfort blanket or favourite toy?
- Do they sleep with the light on?
- Do they like to be rocked to sleep?
- Do they settle all by themselves?

You may want to change some of these things, and this is fine, but you first need to know what they are used to before you go ahead.

Case study
Amber, aged three-and-a-half, and Connor, aged two-and-a-half, were a sister and brother who had been adopted by Pat and Rob about three months ago. Amber was struggling with her sleep.

The situation
These were Pat and Rob's first children. Connor slept in a cot in his new room and had no problems sleeping through the night. Amber slept in a small bed in her own room and had a night light and a safety gate in her bedroom doorway. Despite seeming happy and settled in her new home, she was struggling with being left alone at bedtime, and although her foster carer, who had been looking after both children before the adoption, said that she had always been a good sleeper with her, she had been unsettled and never slept through the night since coming to live with her forever family.

Pat and Rob had blamed this on her anxiety at the change and also to her early experiences: as a baby she had been left alone for long periods. Because of this, they had been giving her lots of reassurance, especially around bedtime. They had got into the habit of one of them (usually Pat) sitting beside her bed as she played on her tablet computer until she went to sleep. Then, later in the night, she would wake up, crying and looking for Pat, and needing her tablet computer again.

The reason for Amber's reluctance to go to sleep alone now may indeed have been caused by the recent changes in her life and her early experiences, but she had up until just a few weeks ago been OK about sleeping alone. Her bedtime behaviour was typical of a young child testing out boundaries, and her night waking and crying, although possibly signs of anxiety, were also typical of any three-year-old child who falls asleep in the company of a parent and then wakes up later to find that they are alone.

The solution
It was decided that Pat and Rob would teach Amber how to settle to sleep at night without either the tablet or one of them sitting beside her. The idea of this made both of them very uncomfortable, as they felt that she needed lots of reassurance and distraction in order to sleep. It was explained that it was, in fact, more traumatic for her to wake up and find herself alone than it would be for her to fall asleep without either of them there in the first place. Provided that they withdrew their presence in a sensitive way, Amber would be OK and she would soon benefit from having better-quality night-time sleep. The family was receiving counselling and support, arranged through the adoption agency, and it was felt that Amber was doing well and seemed to be happy and developing well generally. When I met her, I was struck by her advanced language skills, her relaxed and easy manner with her parents and her outgoing personality.

The sleep plan
- Be confident that Amber has the potential to be a very good sleeper again. Right now she is being held back by her own 'over management' of the bedtime scenario and her reliance on having you close by as she goes to sleep. She then wakes up in the night, is upset that you're no longer there, and needs to find you again.
- Even though she has some natural, age-appropriate fears at bedtime, the main reason she requires the tablet and having you next to her as she sleeps is as much down to habit now rather than emotional need.
- First of all explain to Amber that she is going to do some 'happy sleeping/falling to sleep by herself' and you're going to help her. Tell her that the tablet is going to be kept downstairs at night-time, so that her mind can rest.
- Get an assortment of luminous stars to put on her bedroom wall for good sleeping. Each time she falls asleep without you sitting beside her, in the morning she can have a star to stick on her wall. Once she's earned a star, you should never take one away.
- Bath her and Connor together every night at 7 p.m. After the bath, Rob should take Connor and Pat should take Amber. Encourage a family 'kiss good night'/'See you in the morning!' ritual before they part.

- When you go to her room to settle her for the night, she can have two stories – the first can change each night, but the second one needs to be the same (until her settling problems have resolved). Then have a few minutes of 'golden time' when you talk together about the best bits of your day. After this, make sure that she has everything she needs for the night before you leave her.
- Following this final ritual, kiss her good night and leave the room on a very positive note, 'I'm going to do some jobs. Stay in your bed and I'll be back to see you in two minutes.' Leave the room with confidence.
- If she's wobbly about you leaving, reassure her that you will come back very soon. She can listen to a story tape to help her relax and to occupy her mind, but be strong about not giving the tablet or your phone to her.
- Return to her every few minutes to encourage her and praise her for staying in her bed.
- **If she calls out for you**, tell her that you'll be there in a minute. When you go to her, tell her how good she is for waiting. Don't get involved in any chats or procrastination. You already know that she has all that she needs, so if she asks for anything else, it's OK to say that she can have it in the morning.
- **If she gets out of bed**, you should meet her at the gate and tell her that she needs to be in bed. Take her back to bed quietly and calmly, and then stay with her for a just a few moments to tell her that she needs to stay in bed. There is no need to explain why.
- Then, if she manages to stay in bed, you can keep returning to her every few minutes to encourage her and to reassure her that sleep will soon come.
- If she keeps coming to the gate, and resists you putting her back to bed, then you can leave her at the gate, while you remain upstairs, doing emails or pottering in and out of the bedrooms and on the landing. Make sure that she knows you're around, but you do not have to be within her direct line of vision.
- Return to her every two minutes and offer to help her back to bed. Listen to her requests and acknowledge them but don't comply unless it is truly urgent or she needs to use the toilet or have a drink.
- If she falls asleep on her bedroom floor or by the safety gate, gently carry her to her bed. Sleep will inevitably happen even if she fights it – because her internal body clock will ensure it.

- When she wakes during the night or any time before 7 a.m., go to her quickly but do not ask her what is wrong or why she has woken up. Instead, tell her that it is still sleepy time and remind her that she is going to stay in her own bed. You need to be resolute but not cross. Do the exits and returns as you did earlier – leaving her at the gate if you need to, but for no longer than two minutes at a time before checking her. If she doesn't go back to sleep, just get her up any time after 7 a.m.
- Reassure Connor if he is woken up. One of you should stay with him if necessary.
- Once she's up for the day, she will need lots of positive feedback for sleeping alone. Let her choose a luminous star to put on her bedroom wall.
- Pat should continue to be the one to put Amber to bed for the first three nights, but after that, you can alternate as much as you like.

The outcome

Pat and Rob were nervous about starting what they feared what a might be a harsh solution to Amber's sleep difficulties. They realized, however, that they couldn't continue with the broken nights, which were leaving the whole family, including Amber herself, exhausted during the day.

As it turned out, they did very well at putting the plan into action and sticking with it.

On the first night, Amber was determined to fall asleep as usual, and when Pat stood his ground about her not having the tablet and not sitting beside her as she slept, Amber at one point, shouted, 'Get Rob! He'll sort all this out!'

After that first night of quite severe protest, which included her getting upset that she had the wrong socks on, and asking for Weetabix, Amber began to learn the skills of settling to sleep by herself. Within a week she was settling alone and had stopped waking during the night. She was very happy with and proud of her rewards, and she soon had a lovely constellation on her bedroom wall, which she saw every night and which reminded her of how well she had done.

Conclusion

Even if your child's sleep difficulty is associated with an emotional, medical or situational issue, it is OK to use sensitive techniques to change bedtime behaviour and improve their sleep.

Provided that there other measures in place to address emotional or psychological issues, it is safe and sensible to use a 'behavioural' approach to help solve their sleep problem. This is the case whether it is your adopted child or your birth child.

When it comes to caring for the sleep needs of your adopted child, you – just like any new parent – will need to gather information from books, family, friends and professionals about how to care for them. Armed with this information, you can then start the fabulous process of learning on the job.

Don't be frightened of the fact that they are not your birth child. You are their parent now. You wanted them very much and are getting to know them more every day. Because you are a loving adult and you have their very best interests at heart, you can safely follow your instincts when caring for them. Parenting is a learning process – for both adoptive and birth parents.

Advice for grandparents and other close family members

If you are fortunate enough to have a family that wants to help you with child care, you should *definitely* let them. It's great for both your child and to yourself to have a trusted grandparent or other family member to care for them sometimes. Encouraging your toddler or child to develop close relationships with extended family will be a real benefit and a life-enriching experience for them and it gets them used to the idea of being part of a community. It starts them off on the path to recognizing that they are a member of society in their own right. Not only this, but allowing a grandparent to look after your child will give you a break when you need it and the reassurance to know that you have back-up in case you are ever ill or need to be away from them for work or other reasons.

It is really lovely for your parents to have a child to care for, and provided they are fit and coming to it fresh, the chances are that they will have the energy to cope with your child's needs, even if they are not a brilliant sleeper.

When you arrange for your family member to babysit either in your home or for an overnight stay in theirs, it can take a bit of bravery and confidence to step aside and hand over your child to their care. It will make it easier for everyone if you are really clear about how you would like them to be looked after, and to do so in a respectful way. You might need to accept that a grandparent, with all their years of experience, may have their own ways of settling your child, and provided that their values are broadly in line with your own, this really should not cause any problems. Children from a very young age are able to differentiate and to understand, for example, that, while a grandparent might let them nap in the pram, at home they sleep in their cot.

Tips for happy babysitting

- Let your parent or family member know what your child's usual bedtime routine is like, and what time they can expect them to fall asleep.
- If they are going to your family member's home for a sleepover, send along a familiar bedtime toy or storybook.
- If possible, allow your child to spend time alone with their grandparents during the day before they put them to bed and/or babysit at night.
- If it's the first time for both your child and your parents, stay fairly local, so that you can be home quickly if needed. Your parents will need to feel completely confident that they can care for your child before you go away for the weekend, for example.
- Give them a few ways in which they can contact you while you are out. This isn't a sign of mistrust, but a sensible precaution that increases everyone's confidence.
- Come back at the time that you said you would – not earlier, and not later. This will help to build trust on both sides, too.

8

Additional needs and common physical sleep issues

If your child has additional needs, it is easy to think that if they have sleep problems, it is because of their condition. However, this is only part of them and their sleep picture. There is no need to either let a diagnosis define your child or hold them back from learning how to sleep well.

Autism

It is estimated that about two-thirds of autistic children have problems with sleeping, and there are lots of reasons why this might be the case. The main ones are:

- differences in melatonin production, which affect a child's circadian rhythm
- heightened senses and/or sensory overload
- social cueing problems, which make it difficult for them to make the connection between bedtime routine and bedtime
- anxiety
- associated neurological problems like epilepsy
- food allergies/sensitivities/issues which are common in children with autism spectrum disorders (ASDs), causing digestive problems and discomfort.
- other, associated health issues which can cause them discomfort and/or pain.

If your toddler or child is autistic, one sleep problem that you might experience is difficulty in establishing a regular bedtime, due to their naturally irregular or random sleep/wake patterns. They might want to sleep all day and then be ready to party at night, when everyone else wants to go to bed. Associated with this is them having difficulty settling off to sleep and a delayed sleep onset, which, as we have seen, can be common in lots of children. Because of the difference in melatonin production, some autistic children sleep in short bursts rather than for a sustained period, and this of course can mean lots of night wakings and sometimes very early waking as well.

It is so important to address and try to resolve any sleep issues rather than just accepting them as part of your child's difference. You want your child to be as well-equipped as possible to enjoy their life, their education and their friendships. We know that poor sleep in younger autistic children can lead to an increase in such things as social difficulties, struggles with learning and challenging behaviours.

Just a reminder about the all-important sleep hormone, melatonin. It is this hormone that puts us to sleep and keeps us asleep. However, in people with autism, its production can be low or irregular. **However, as we discussed earlier, behavioural factors or measures can often override biological barriers.** To help your child maximize their melatonin production, there are practical (behavioural) and natural things you can do:

- Encourage daylight exposure.
- Stop screen time one hour before bedtime.
- Have lots of exercise during the day.
- Keep lights low one hour before bedtime.
- Keep a low red night light in the bedroom – all night.
- Use blackout blinds during the summer months.

Encourage foods which contain tryptophan (milk, chicken, turkey, nuts, oats, tuna, nuts and seeds, and CHOCOLATE (yes!). **Tryptophan** is an amino acid that helps melatonin production.

If your autistic child has sleep problems, you may have been prescribed some synthetic melatonin by your paediatrician. Synthetic melatonin should be given only as a short-term measure, and always along with some practical support and guidance about helping your child get into a good bedtime routine. It can be helpful for some children, especially if it is used to help kick-start a new sleep plan – once a new sleep behaviour is established, the melatonin can be withdrawn.

Prescribed melatonin is usually given about 30 minutes to one hour before bedtime, and it can help a child to fall asleep. Unlike natural melatonin which continues to be produced during the night, the synthetic melatonin wears off quite quickly, and this can of course cause them to wake in the night. *However,* if you are able to take advantage of the prescribed melatonin at bedtime and use its effect to help you teach your child how to fall asleep in their own bed, without having you sitting right next to them, this alone can help them to resettle more easily without you, if and when they wake up later.

In addition to the measures that you can take increase your child's sleep hormone (melatonin) levels, there are other things that you can do to create the ideal conditions for them to sleep. These can be separated into three categories:

Biological	Environmental	Behavioural
• The appropriate awake window so that they have built up enough sleep pressure to sleep. • A healthy amount of melatonin in their system.	• A tidy room – put toys away before bedtime. • A dark room or a dim red night light to encourage melatonin production.	• A familiar recognizable bedtime routine. • A Social Story™ to help prepare for changes to the way that they sleep.

Biological	Environmental	Behavioural
• Not being overtired – i.e. keeping their cortisol levels low. • To be well fed but not overfull; give food high in tryptophan (see above). • Avoid sweets/cola/fizzy drinks and foods with artificial colouring and other chemical additives.	• Have the walls and furnishings in soft, muted colours. • Thick carpets to muffle sounds. • White noise/noise-cancelling headphones. • Try sensory lighting – lava lamp/bubble lamp/fibre-optic lamp (red tones). • Avoid strong food smells etc. • Have your child fall asleep in the same conditions that they then subsequently wake up to. • Some people use a weighted blanket, with the belief that they good for sensory processing issues and can provide a sense of calm. It should be said that most sleep experts don't believe in their effectiveness, and they should *never* be used for very young children.	• To fall asleep alone, so that they don't wake later feeling upset that you've gone. It's fine to do this in gradual steps – altering the social story as you go. • Rewards for good sleeping.

In the table I mention the use of a Social Story™ to help an autistic child improve the way that they sleep. Social Stories were created by Carol Gray in 1991. They are short, simple stories that help a person deal with certain situations, activities or events. They give information about what to expect in that situation. Parents can find out more about how to use Social Stories by visiting the National Autistic Society website (https://www.autism.org.uk/) or https://carolgraysocialstories.com.

I use Social Stories a lot in my work with children with special needs, and they are very effective as well as being fun for the child.

Case study

A four-year-old boy with autism, Krish, co-sleeping with his parents and learning to make the transition to sleep in his own bed.

The situation

Krish was a four-year-old boy with autism who loved cars. He lived with his mum and dad, Arjun and Riyal, and his 18-month-old sister, Kiya. He slept in the same bed as his parents at night, but had recently been given a racing car bed of his own.

Kiya, who was developing typically, slept all night in a cot in her own room. Arjun tended to be the parent who put Krish to bed at night, and Riyal usually settled Kiya.

Krish attended a special-needs nursery school, and he had a sensory room at home. He loved to play on his tablet computer, especially in the evening after dinner, and doing so helped him to relax. He also loved to play with his toy cars.

He had dropped his daytime nap nearly a year previously.

His parents wanted him to sleep in his own bed, as he was getting bigger and he was very active in his sleep, which was affecting the quality of their own sleep. They still wanted to have him close by, and they were happy to all share the same room.

The solution

Krish's parents needed a clear and supportive plan to help him make the transition to his own bed, and once he was there, all of them would sleep better. It was decided to use a Social Story to introduce him to the idea of sleeping at night in his own bed and for the parents to use a Friday night to make the move. This way, if they had a bad couple of nights, they would be able to take turns in catching up with sleep during the day.

The sleep plan

- Put Krish's pillow into his racing car bed. Show him that is where he will be sleeping.
- Using photographs of him and the family, and your home, make a storybook for him, using the following text:

> My name is Krish.
> I like cars and I have a big red car bed.
> At bedtime I put my computer away.
> I have my bath with my sister, Kiya.
> I say good night to Kiya.
> I put on my pyjamas.
> I have my milk and clean my teeth.
> I like to cuddle Daddy before I get into bed.
> I sleep in my car bed now.
> 'Night-night, Mummy. See you in the morning!'
> 'Night-night, Daddy. See you in the morning!'
> I sleep all night in my car bed.
> Hurrah, Krish!

Start his bedtime routine at about 7 p.m. Bath him with Kiya, and after this encourage the children to kiss good night. and as usual take Krish to the lounge and let him play with his cars for a few minutes as you get his milk ready.

Give his milk in the lounge while looking at his personal story with you.

Then go to the bathroom to clean his teeth and afterwards go directly to the bedroom. Arjun should cuddle Krish for a few minutes while sitting on the racing car bed.

Kiss good night to Mummy, then kiss good night to Daddy and place him in his car bed. Mummy can lie on the big bed, and Daddy stay beside Krish.

If he wants to go in the big bed with mummy, let him do so for a few minutes and then take him back to the racing car bed, with lots of encouragement. Let him know how proud you are when he is in his own bed.

It may take over an hour for Krish to settle in his own bed on the first night, and there could be a few trips from bed to bed. Give him as long as he needs and wait it out until he falls asleep eventually in his own bed.

In the night, if Krish wakes, you can go to him and reassure him. Tell him that it is still time for sleep and he is doing so well in his racing car bed. Don't have him back in your bed to sleep, as this could become a nightly habit. It is best to cuddle him on his bed again if he needs it, and then keep trying to put him back to sleep. It will be tough at first but will very soon get better.

Potentially, you could be up for most of the night with him, but please stay calm and stick with this, as he won't be able to change to his own bed without your help.

Any disruption to your own sleep will just be *very* temporary, and soon you will *all* benefit as Krish will sleep better in own bed.

When you get him up for the day, give him plenty of praise, cuddles and affection and keep your praise as honest and specific as you can – 'Krish, you slept in your car bed!'

The outcome

Krish surprised everyone by very happily sleeping in his car bed from the first night! His parents had been concerned that he would struggle, but in fact he was used to seeing his racing car bed in the bedroom, and he liked it. When they moved his pillow there and did the story about how he was going to sleep in his own bed, he was absolutely fine with it!

He welcomed the praise in the morning, which reinforced the good feelings that he had had about his bed and him sleeping in his own bed, very quickly became the norm. Arjun and Riyal slept much better in their bed without Krish and as a result, they had more energy in the daytime. This meant that they were able to do more fun things with both of their children, and everyone benefitted.

Conclusion

Social Stories are a great tool that parents can use to help *all* children cope with change, but they are especially useful for children with special needs.

Attention deficit and hyperactivity disorder (ADHD)

ADHD is a condition that often runs in families and affects a person's behaviour. The symptoms are:

- trouble paying attention
- forgetfulness

- being impulsive
- being hyperactive.

Because these symptoms are also normal for toddlers, a child is not usually given a diagnosis of ADHD until they've started school.

The very interesting thing about the signs and symptoms of ADHD is that they are virtually identical to those associated with a lack of sleep. In fact, many children who have been thought to have had ADHD turn out to be perfectly OK when they are helped to improve their sleep. We know, too, that there is a link between sleep-related breathing disorders and ADHD. Children who have the condition have a higher-than-usual chance of being a snorer, having large adenoids or experiencing sleep apnoea.

Around 70 per cent of children who have ADHD will have difficulties with switching off and falling asleep, and others will experience problems like night waking and early-morning waking.

So the relationship between sleep and ADHD is complex and important. If you have a child who you or others suspect has ADHD, then one of your first priorities should be to help get them some more sleep ... and I know that is not as easy to do as it sounds.

You child will need to have a gold-standard bedtime routine! All of the things that we have discussed in this book which help a child to sleep well are *especially* important.

Top ten tips for helping children with ADHD get the sleep that they need

1 A *super*-regular sleep/wake schedule. Wake them by 8 a.m. each morning, even if they have had a bad night.
2 Don't let them sleep too late in the afternoon (even if it's tempting for you to have some quiet time to yourself).

3 Provided that they haven't napped (or they've napped before 3 p.m. if they are still very young), put them to bed at the same time each night. Ideally, this would be between 7 p.m. and 8 p.m.

4 Follow a highly structured and familiar bedtime routine, and make sure that you are the one in charge!

5 Have their bedroom calm, dark and quiet.

6 Consider making a Social Story™ to let them understand how to stay in their bed and fall asleep.

7 Avoid any night-time rituals such as getting into your bed, which will inadvertently give them the message that their own bed is just a temporary 'holding pen'.

8 Give rewards and specific praise for good sleeping.

9 If you know that your child has certain 'trigger foods' that make their symptoms worse, you should avoid these.

10 Seek medical help for issues such as tonsils, adenoids, snoring and sleep apnoea or other breathing issues.

Cerebral palsy (CP) and other neuromuscular difficulties

There are many reasons why a toddler or young child with cerebral palsy might have difficulties with their sleep. The main ones are:

- physical discomfort and positioning for sleep
- digestive problems such as constipation and reflux
- muscle spasms
- breathing difficulties associated with scoliosis
- not understanding sleep cues if they have a learning difference
- choking and swallowing difficulties
- medical conditions such as epilepsy.

When you have your hospital or clinic appointments to review your child's needs, discussions about their sleep should be as important as discussions around their medical care, nutrition and other needs. Children with CP really benefit from a team approach to help them with their sleeping – for example:

- their physiotherapist can help with positioning for their comfortable and safe sleeping;
- their paediatrician can ensure that all of the medical aspects such as control of epilepsy or muscle spasms are being properly treated;
- their occupational therapist can help with sensory issues affecting their sleep;
- their dietitian can advise about the right nutrition to support your child and their sleeping.

Once all that is covered, you will then give your child all the simple, behavioural cues that we have discussed so far in this book, to help them as far as possible to learn how to fall asleep under their own steam and resettle to sleep when they naturally stir in their sleep.

Visual impairment

Our body's circadian master clock, which helps us to sleep at night and be wakeful in the day, depends largely on us being able to experience light. This light perception controls the rate and release of melatonin, the sleep hormone.

Toddlers with a visual impairment, especially those who are profoundly blind, will usually experience problems with their circadian rhythm, meaning that they can be up at night and then want to sleep in the day. This can have a detrimental effect, not only on them in terms of their health and social development, but also on their parents.

It is so important that, rather than just going along with things and accepting being up all night as inevitable, you do something about it.

Your doctor is likely to prescribe synthetic melatonin to help your child to sleep, and while this can be helpful, there are other things that you can do to help. First, while perception of light is the main thing that sets the circadian clock, it is not the *only* thing. Maintaining a very regular daytime schedule for getting up, having meals, exercise, socializing and sharing stories can really help. These consistent time cues – called zeitgebers ('time givers') – can help to set your child's internal body clock to sleep at night.

Sleep tips to help if your child has a visual impairment

- Try prescribed melatonin but don't rely on it as the only thing to help your child to sleep.
- Drop the daytime nap as soon as your child starts to resist it. In your case, dropping the nap early is a good thing.
- Have a rock-solid *daytime* routine as well as a *bedtime* routine.
- Take meals at the same time each day, and do planned activities at the same each day, too. It might seem a bit unspontaneous, but it's good for the zeitgebers!
- If your child is able to perceive light, spend as much possible outside in the daytime or in the brightest room in the house.
- Use voice cues to indicate the time of day. Speak in a quiet voice for bedtime and night-time: 'It's night-time, darling. We are all going to sleep.' In the daytime, use a bright voice: 'It's daytime, and we're all awake! Soon we are going to play in the garden!'
- Use meal cues. Have meals at set times, and tell your child what meal it is: 'Good morning, it's breakfast time!'; 'We've finished at playgroup now, and it's time for lunch'; 'It's getting late now, and it's time for our dinner/tea.'

Down's syndrome

At least half of all children who have Down's syndrome also have difficulties with sleeping. Their sleep problems are mainly caused by:

- obstructive sleep apnoea – which is *very* common in children who have Down's syndrome and is often caused or worsened by tonsils, adenoids blocking their airway, which may be already restricted due to a larger tongue;
- particular and characteristic sleep disturbances which are associated with Down's syndrome and are not necessarily linked to the sleep apnoea – these include extra movements in the night, more wakings, comparatively less REM (dream) sleep and more deep sleep;
- behavioural issues such as difficulty in establishing boundaries.

Most commonly, sleep problems are caused by a mixture of all three of these factors.

Obstructive sleep apnoea (OSA) is when breathing is disturbed or pauses when someone falls asleep, and their throat relaxes allowing the airway to become narrowed or blocked. It is common in adults, and it can happen in children, too – particularly, but not always, in children who have Down's syndrome.

Sometimes a child can stop breathing several times in the night, and even though they won't stop breathing permanently, because the body sends a response to the brain which causes them to semi wake up and breathe again, this is a serious condition and it shouldn't be ignored. It can have an impact on your child's health and wellbeing, as well as their learning, behaviour and mood.

Often, having tonsils and adenoids will resolve OSA but sometimes affected children will need to receive continuous positive air pressure (CPAP) via a soft mask which looks like a small oxygen mask, and covers their nose and sometimes their mouth, too. It is connected via a tube to a device next to the child's bed or cot which delivers a stream of air at a constant, moderate pressure and keeps the airway open. This totally stops the OSA and can have a transformative effect on the quality of their sleep.

Children with Down's syndrome, in common with all children who have learning differences, are really helped to maximize their sleep potential, by having a particularly structured bedtime routine with clear boundaries and lots of repetition. Rewards and praise for independent sleeping are especially effective.

At the time of writing, the UK charity Scope (https://www.scope.org.uk) offers free help from trained sleep practitioners to children who have disabilities, as do various other charities, such as The Sleep Charity (https://thesleepcharity.org.uk). It can be hard enough sometimes to establish good sleep skills when your toddler is typically developing, and when you're unsure about the implications for sleep when your child has additional needs, it is even more challenging. Friends and family may help and advise you, and hopefully the information in this book will give you confidence; but if you are struggling, you can speak with your child's consultant, GP, therapist or health visitor for a referral to your local paediatric sleep services or the relevant charity. Your child needs their sleep, and so do you – this is not a luxury treatment that you're seeking, and getting sleep help should be a priority.

Common physical sleep problems

Snoring

It is not at all unusual for a child to occasionally snore during sleep, as they have such small nasal passages. These little airways can easily become over-congested, especially during periods of teething or colds, causing them to snore.

Snoring can sometimes be a sign of allergies, and if you suspect that your child is allergic to something in the environment, you should avoid feather bedding and do your best to keep the room free from dust and pet hairs. Dietary allergies can also cause snoring, and you may be able to notice a link between certain foods that your child has eaten and their level of snoring.

Other causes of snoring are enlarged adenoids and tonsils, being overweight, asthma and sometimes a child having a particular anatomical or facial structure, like the characteristic features of a child with Down's syndrome or a deviated septum, a cleft palate or a small, receding chin, for example.

If your child's snoring happens occasionally and is quite mild, then it is probably harmless. But sometimes snoring can be a sign of a more serious problem, especially if it is loud or stops and starts, or if your child seems to pant, gasp or stop breathing during sleep. These things indicate that they could have a sleep breathing disorder caused by obstructive sleep apnoea, which we discussed above, and which, if present, will need treatment.

If your child snores regularly, more than a couple of times a week, and if the snoring is severe enough to disturb their regular breathing, then you should seek advice from your doctor.

Otherwise, for occasional, light snoring, a humidifier or boiled kettle in the room (carefully watched and removed when your child enters the room) can help to relieve a stuffy nose. A drink of water kept next to the bed might be needed if they have a dry mouth when they can't breathe through their nose.

Rocking and banging

About two-thirds of children demonstrate some kind of 'sleep-related rhythmic movements' as they fall asleep at bedtime and then again if they wake in the night. These can be body rolling, head rolling or even head banging – and are the ways that lots of children like to settle themselves to sleep. Some children make loud humming or other noises, and this is also a way of them self-soothing. All of these night-time movements, while they may be noisy and disruptive to the family, are almost always harmless for the child concerned. Although some children with differences such as autism may bang their heads, head-banging and rhythmic movement alone is not a sign of autism. Neither is it a sign of emotional distress or illness, and provided that they are not hurting themselves and are developing typically, you can relax and wait for them to grow out of it. This usually happens by the time they are five years old, but often it is earlier.

Teeth grinding

Teeth grinding, or **bruxism**, to give it its medical term, is another kind of behaviour which is associated with sleep. Whereas in adults, it can be a sign of stress, in children, teeth grinding is more likely to be related to their dentition and to helping the top and bottom teeth to become aligned. Most children grind their teeth at some point, and although it can be very noisy and can have the same cringey effect as nails down a blackboard, it is harmless from the child's point of view. It happens mostly when children are in the deepest sleep of the night, so perhaps you've heard them doing it before you go to bed yourself. If it is really bothering you, you can reposition your child to rouse them slightly and this might stop the teeth grinding, but it would be a mistake to wake them up fully.

Sleeping when a child is poorly

Minor illnesses

On average, toddlers and preschoolers have about 6–12 minor illnesses such as viruses, colds and tummy upsets each year. Exposure to antigens in young childhood builds up their immune system, and so, even though these illnesses can be tough at the time to cope with, they do actually make your child's resistance to infections stronger in the long run.

When your child is unwell with minor illness, it is good to follow your normal bedtime routine as closely as possible. Be aware that they may be irritated or uncomfortable at being handled, especially if they are in pain or feel achy. Before bath time you might consider giving a dose of junior paracetamol/acetaminophen (in the US and some other countries) or ibuprofen to control their pain and keep their temperature down before they go to sleep. Many parents prefer to give ibuprofen at bedtime, as it is long acting but needs to be taken when there is something in a child's tummy, and then, if a second dose of painkiller is needed during the night, to give paracetamol/acetaminophen, which is gentler on an emptier stomach. Paracetamol/acetaminophen and ibuprofen are from two different families of painkillers and because of that, in circumstances when pain and raised temperature are severe, they can be given in tandem. Your pharmacist, health visitor or GP practice/family doctor can advise you about this, and because any medication needs to taken with care, especially when it comes to young children, there are always instructions available on the labels that you need to read carefully.

Contrary to what many people think, these painkillers do not contain any sedative and will not cause your child to feel sleepy or dozy. The virus or illness may cause them to feel sleepy, however, and if this is the case, you should let them sleep as much as they need to. Sleep is a great healer.

Insight: Cytokines

During night-time sleep, there is an increase in the production of cytokines. These are proteins which act as messengers for the immune system. When your child sleeps, their immune system 'remembers' how to recognize and react to dangerous antigens. This helps them to resist and to fight infections.

After their bath time, offer a bedtime drink or, if they are still having it, a milk feed. Don't be too stressed if your child refuses their usual milk or doesn't take it all. If they are poorly, they are very unlikely to wake up hungry, even if they haven't eaten much during the day. Their body needs to rest and repair at night-time, and if they have lost their appetite, they will soon regain it and catch up with any lost calories when they are better.

If your child usually self-settles, you should allow them to go to sleep without help, as usual. It's fine to return frequently to them to check and reassure them, but rocking them to sleep can become a difficult habit to break once they are better.

If they wake up in the night and are clearly unwell, you should go to them, pick them up or sit them up if necessary and offer a drink of water (not milk – even if they didn't have it at bedtime). These actions alone can help to unblock the nose and the small tubes connecting the back of the nose to the ears, helping your child to feel more comfortable. If they continue crying, and/or if they feel hot, you can give a dose of infant painkiller, provided that it is a different family of painkiller than that which they had at bedtime. Or if it *is* the same one as at bedtime, you carefully follow the instructions supplied, concerning the timing and spacing of doses.

You can then remain close by until they are calm and settled. Tempting as it might be, it is best if you avoid bringing them into bed with you if they are poorly, and especially if they have a high temperature. If you need to watch over them, it is safer and better for their sleep long term for you to go and sleep in their bedroom instead.

Insight
It usually takes two or three consecutive nights of your child coming into your bed, being given a night feed again or being rocked to sleep, for instance, for these behaviours to become habitual again.

Of course, sometimes it is unavoidable that you will relax the usual routines around bedtime when they are unwell. As soon as they are better, however, you need to allow them to self-settle at the start of the night, drop the night cuddles, and let them get back to sleeping as they did before the illness.

Longer-term illnesses

When a child who has a longer-term illness struggles with their sleep, it can be really tricky to work out whether the sleeplessness is caused by the illness or whether it is caused by habit. This dilemma is one that is shared by not only parents, but often medical professionals, too. If there is any doubt, it is wiser and kinder of course to err on the side of caution and address or blame the illness.

However, if you feel that your child is suffering from a lack of sleep, and that their medical condition is made worse by this, or that tiredness is making it more difficult for your child to cope with their illness, it makes sense to do your best to help them improve their sleep.

Pain

Sadly, some children suffer from chronic or intermittent pain, caused by a variety of conditions and medical treatments. It is absolutely vital that pain is treated effectively and that you discuss all possible options with your doctor or specialist. Treatment for pain need not always be with painkilling medicines (although, if these are recommended, it is always good to follow your doctor's advice). Often, things such as massage, positioning, warm baths and complementary therapies can be very useful in the treatment of painful conditions.

Once you are confident that your child's pain is under control at bedtime, it is the perfect time to teach them how to sleep fall asleep independently. **If their sleep skills at the start of the night are well established and strong, they will be better able to join their sleep cycles at night, and it is more likely that they will be able to sleep through any minor pain that they might experience during the night.**

'Cry it out' techniques are not usually appropriate for children who are unwell, especially if they experience pain. It is more acceptable, kind and sensible to withdraw more gradually at the beginning of, and during, the night. See Chapter 10 for a choice and description of the available techniques.

Asthma

Some longer-term medical conditions, such as asthma when it's not well controlled, are often worse during the night, when a child is lying down. Coughing can also cause night waking, of course. As with pain control, it is important that children receive the best possible treatment to control their symptoms. Some of the medicines and inhalers used to open up a child's airways can also have a stimulating effect on them. With this in mind, if this kind of medicine is given on a regular basis (rather than just being given as needed), it is better to give it earlier in the day. If your child is wheezy before bed and needs the medicine, then, of course, it is essential to prioritize their breathing over their sleeping.

If your child has difficulty in breathing, or has a tendency to cough during the night, there are certain practical steps that you can take to keep them comfortable:

- Avoid your child coming into contact with tobacco smoke, both during the day and at night. Don't allow anyone to smoke in your home, even if they are downstairs and your child is upstairs.
- Tilt up the top of the cot or bed by placing thick books under the feet of the cot/bed.
- Use a humidifier in the bedroom or, if you don't have one, boil a kettle in there for several minutes before they go to bed. (Remove it before they come into the room.)
- Use menthol or eucalyptus either in a humidifier or vaporizer. Over the age of two years, it is OK to use a mild menthol rub on their chest or menthol drops on their vest or pyjamas.
- Have a drink of water close to hand, to ease any coughing during the night.

In common with children who have pain, it is important to teach children with breathing problems how to go to sleep independently at the beginning of the night. If you are able to do this, it will strengthen their ability to settle if they wake up during the night. After attending to your child after a coughing or wheezing episode during the night, you will both be very tired. It is best that your child is able to resettle once they are comfortable again, and that they don't rely on coming into your bed or you sleeping on their floor or in their bed as they go back to sleep – unless they are so unwell that they need watching over.

Eczema

If your toddler had eczema as a baby and hasn't yet grown out of it, it is likely that now it has moved to their elbow creases and knee creases. They may also have it on their wrists, hands and ankles, as well as around their mouth and on their eyelids.

The most common type of eczema in children is **atopic eczema/dermatitis**, and this is linked to allergies. If your child has atopic eczema, there is a chance that at some time their sleep is going to be affected by it. The most disruptive aspect of eczema on sleep is the itching and the desire to scratch. As a parent of a child with eczema, you will know that, if they have spent the night awake and scratching, their skin can be really damaged by morning. For this reason, it is natural that, when you know that they are awake, you will want to step in and help them go back to sleep without scratching. The problem with this is that, if you end up staying with them as they go to sleep, they are very likely then to wake in the night, upset that you've gone!

Tips for managing eczema and sleep

- Bath them every night in warm (not hot) water, to which an emollient has been added. The bath will keep the skin clean, remove dead cells and old creams and emollients. It will also warm and soften the skin, making it ready and more absorbent for fresh moisturizers and any topical steroids or other medical applications such as protopic creams.
- Pat them gently dry with a towel, rather than rubbing them and damaging their skin or triggering the itch–scratch–itch cycle.
- If your child is tempted to scratch, teach them how to tap on or pat their itchy skin instead. This can stop the itch without damaging the skin.
- Use pure cotton clothing and bedding, and keep the room cool.
- If they want a comfort toy, use one that is cotton and washable, rather than a plush teddy bear. Have two of them, so that you can wash one while the other is being used.
- Use a non-biological washing powder, and avoid fabric conditioner. Machine-wash your child's clothing, and at the end of the wash, run an extra rinse cycle.
- Vacuum and damp dust their room regularly, and use simple cotton curtains or blinds, rather than heavy drapes. Similarly, avoid upholstered furniture and stick to plain wood or plastic.

Going into hospital

The disruption of either a single or frequent hospital admissions can sometimes have a negative impact on your child's ability to sleep. Often, their sleep will be disturbed by a constant level of light, which limits their body's ability to recognize daytime and night-time cues and affects their production of the sleep hormone, melatonin. On top of this, they may need to be woken up at night for medical observation, to be given medicine or for other treatments. Their normal bedtime routine will, of course, be disrupted, and your child will lose the benefit of the familiar environmental cues that indicate that it is time for sleep.

While you are in hospital with your child, the most important thing is that you make both them and yourself as comfortable as possible. Take as many familiar items with a night-time association from home as you can. Especially important are those things that you use for bedtime, such as a familiar teddy or night-time book. If you are able to bath your child, it is good to do this before bed (even though bedtime might be later than usual) and use as many familiar verbal sleep triggers from your home bedtime routine as you can. These include the familiar bath-time song that you sing, good-night phrases and so on.

Take heart in the fact that children are able to recognize that there are different settling 'rules' when away from home from the normal ones. Those who sleep well and settle without problems at home will usually settle back into their usual sleep routine and habits once they are back in their own familiar environment.

9

Understanding why your child is struggling with sleep, and preparing for change

As we talked about in Chapter 1, it is completely normal for toddlers, young children and indeed all of us to wake in the night – especially in the small hours when cortisol levels naturally rise in preparation for the day. The problem isn't that they wake up, but rather that they wake and can't get back to sleep without help.

It is possible for you to identify why your child is not resettling when they wake up if you look at the main causes for this. You might want to see if there are any comparisons that you can make or if any of these reasons reflect your situation.

Top ten reasons for children not resettling when they wake in the night

1 Being over helped to go to sleep at the start of the night. If you sit or lie next to your child, as they fall asleep, they will be upset when they wake up later and you are no longer there.

2 Falling asleep on the sofa, your bed, the car, and so on, and then being moved to their bed while they are asleep. If they fall asleep on a regular basis in one place and then wake to find themselves in another, they will be upset and disoriented when they wake later.

3 Waking to find that their familiar sleep cues have gone or their surroundings in the room have changed. If your child falls asleep holding a bottle of milk, or falls asleep to music, story

recordings, TV, tablet, or a night light on, and if when they are asleep you remove these props or cues, when they wake up they will feel like something is wrong.

4 **Expecting some kind of ritual of contact with you either during the night or at dawn (which they might think is night).** This could be any familiar action, but most commonly the expected ritual would be a breast feed, a bottle of milk, a cuddle, some medicine or getting into your bed. If your child has an early-morning transfer to your bed (which they think is night), this may be causing them to regard their own cot or bed as just a temporary resting place until they get into their rightful place beside you! Equally, the expectations of night feeds could be causing them to wake up. As we know, toddlers and young children don't need night feeds for nutritional reasons, but many keep them going out of habit rather than need. Look back at Chapter 4 for more advice.

5 **Discomfort, such as teething, or feeling hot, cold or in pain, or having a soaked or dirty nappy.** Sometimes these things can cause night waking, but I find in my work with families that parents very often are too quick to look to these physical causes for their child's wakefulness and miss the behavioural causes above (numbers 1–4) which are *far* more likely to be causing the problem!

6 **Incorrect naps and timings.** When a child drops their nap, they can become overtired at bedtime. Overtiredness causes a rise in cortisol and adrenaline levels which then leads to broken nights and/or early waking. When a child has too much daytime sleep or sleeps too late in the day, this can cause them to have difficulty in falling asleep at bedtime. This in turn can lead to bedtime procrastination, poor sleep associations and sleep onset delay.

7 **Too much screen time and not enough natural daylight exposure.** Daylight exposure sets a child's internal clock to sleep at night. It encourages the production of sleep hormones and also 'feel good' hormones such as serotonin. Overexposure to screens inhibits the release of sleep hormones and gives children a false energy when they are tired.

8 **Nightmares, night terrors and other disorders of arousal.** Despite having good sleep routines in place, these can sometimes still

happen, and your child will need you to support them if and when they do. If you respond well (see Chapter 4), you can minimize the effects of these night-time disturbances.

9 **Thinking it is morning!** Keeping your child's room nice and dark is good for their melatonin production, but being in a permanently blacked-out room can sometimes cause confusion as to when it's daytime and when it's night-time. With older toddlers and preschoolers, the use of daytime signifiers such as pre-set lamps and sleep training clocks can be very helpful. With younger toddlers, simply opening the curtains, putting on the light and changing the tone of your voice from 'night mode' to 'day mode' can give them these clues that help them differentiate night from day.

10 **Heightened emotions.** Anxiety, excitement, worry and stress can sometimes cause a child to have broken nights, just as it does for adults.

For most children with sleep problems, one or more of the above reasons will be the cause. If you can establish what is *causing* your child's sleep difficulties, then you're halfway to *solving* them!

Getting ready for change

There is no doubt at all that some children are better sleepers than others. You might be a parent of more than one child and have never had problems with your older or younger ones. Your bedtime routine with your sleepless child may be just the same as it was with the others, so why are you having a problem now? The fact is that all children are individuals, and while, for example, falling asleep over a night-time bottle will not cause later waking problems for some toddlers, for others it is a recipe for night-time disaster.

You are about to change the way that you approach bedtime practices with your sleepless child, but this does not mean that what you have been doing previously has been wrong. **It is just that it is wrong for them right now.**

Don't forget, either, that some of the habits that you established to settle your child when they were younger, and which were appropriate at the time, may now be working against you. The prime example of this is continuing to pat or soothe your child to sleep or giving night feeds when they are no longer nutritionally necessary.

It can be very daunting even to contemplate the prospect of tackling your child's sleep problem. You may be worried that changing the routine that they are used to will upset them, and if you're already walking around on eggshells with them, the thought of not doing things as they want might feel a bit frightening. It is hard work coping with your toddler's needs during the day, in terms of offering them interesting things to do, making meals, giving cuddles, and so on. You may well be doing this as well as working in a paid job and/or looking after your older or younger children, too. By the time it gets to bedtime, most parents, quite understandably, are tempted to take the line of least resistance. If your nights with your toddler are bad, then the prospect of them getting worse can be an unbearable thought.

Remember, though, that if your nights are already difficult, you have little to lose.

Some reassurance if you are dealing with criticism for teaching your toddler to sleep alone

At the back of your mind you might worry that, by taking control of your child's sleep, you will be harming them emotionally. Of course, you aware of the very powerful parenting voice, especially present on social media that says that it is normal for children to wake in the night, that they are not 'broken' and don't need 'fixing'; that parenting is not a 7 a.m. to 7 p.m. job and that you have a duty to be there around the clock for your child. All of this is true, of course – it *is* normal for children to wake in the night, and you *do* need to be there for them when they need you – but it is a shame to perpetuate and reinforce a child's night-time disruption when it is happening out of habit rather than need. There is a loving and sensible middle ground, and you should not feel guilty about helping your child to improve the quality of their night-time sleep. Guidance, boundaries and direction are important for young children, and you can help them learn how to sleep using an approach which is responsive and loving. Making a positive decision to do something about your child's and family's sleep takes more effort, thought and confidence than simply going with the flow.

If you are a parent who *does* go with the flow when it comes to your child's sleeping, if this is truly your natural parenting style, and you are all happy, rested and healthy, then that's fabulous and you don't need to do anything. You do not have to justify your approach, and you should not feel guilty. Equally, if you want to have a routine where your child is enabled to go to bed in the evening and sleep through the night alone until morning, then you should not be made to feel guilty, either. Parenting is a challenging enough job as it is without other people criticizing you and knocking your confidence.

I've found over the years that sleep problems can arise when couples *disagree* about their parenting styles or when one parent feels overburdened with the responsibility of their child's sleep needs. When a child is not sleeping well, inevitably one or both parents' sleep will suffer as a result. The outcome can have a dreadful effect on any relationship and can affect your working and social life too.

Typical points of difficulty and conflict arise under the following circumstances:

- One parent carries their own memories from a childhood in which they were left to cry a lot. This will, of course, influence their feelings about how their own child should be cared for.
- A parent has witnessed friends or family adopting a more laid-back approach to their baby's sleep which has involved baby co-sleeping and/or staying up very late with the parents instead of being asleep in their own cot. One parent might love this approach, while the other one is horrified by it!
- Parents are over-influenced by either sleep 'gurus' or family and friends, which affects their confidence.
- Just one parent is able to settle the child for sleep. This is almost always a matter of association and habit on the part of the child rather than genuine preference, but it can leave both parents feeling frustrated and resentful.
- There are cultural and ideological differences about parents' roles – often with the wage earner insisting that the stay-at-home parent keep the child quiet at all costs during the night.
- On the matter of bed sharing, having your toddler in bed with you will usually affect your sexual relationship. Lots of people don't feel like having sex with their partner for some considerable time after the birth of a child (for many reasons!). In time the child can become almost like a shield as protection from unwanted sexual advances.

One of the keys to getting a child's sleep right has to start with open and honest communication between parents. As a children's sleep specialist, I find that parents' views and experience of a sleep problem can be hugely different. It is very important that each understand the other's point of view so that a realistic picture of their child's sleep and the way to improve it is clearly understood and accepted by both of you.

Keeping a sleep diary

Before commencing a sleep programme of any kind, it is a really good idea to keep a diary of your child's sleep for a typical week. The diary doesn't have to be complicated but it should be completed honestly and be written up as close to the time as possible. If both you and your partner take it in turns to attend to your child in the night, you both need to fill in the diary.

A sleep diary will reveal:

- a realistic overview of your child's sleep
- the times when they are actually ready to sleep
- whether there is a relationship between certain nap times/ activities and their sleep
- under what conditions they are likely to sleep best
- what (if any) their sleep triggers are.

Keeping the diary might highlight an obvious cause for their poor sleep – for example, over-napping during the day leading to settling problems at bedtime. If this is the case, the solution is easy – you just need to adjust or drop the daytime nap. No formal sleep training will be necessary.

Sometimes the mere action of keeping a diary will help you – just by facing the situation as it is, honestly and realistically. Keeping the diary can have a direct and positive influence on the way you address your baby's sleep needs. By adopting a more organized approach, you might find that you solve your child's sleep problem without even knowing that you are doing it.

Your diary should be tailored to reflect your child and the family. For example, you would only need to document your child's daytime mealtimes and food intake if they are feeding in the night. Feel free to design the layout and content of your personal sleep diary, but here is an example that you might like to use.

Sample sleep diary

Starting the day • Morning wake-up time • Where they woke, e.g. in their bed/cot/your bed • Mood on waking • Getting-up time • First activity of the day, e.g. into your bed/up for breakfast	
• **During the day** • Time, length and place of nap(s) • How you settled them to sleep • How long it took	
• **Food and drink taken** • Meals • Snacks • How much milk?	
• **Bedtime** • Time bedtime routine started • Time went to sleep • How they settled to sleep • Where they fell asleep, e.g. in their bed cot/in your arms • Where you were when they slept	
• **During the night** • Times and length of waking • What you did to resettle them • Night feeds – time(s), number, duration/amount	

What kind of a sleep problem does your child have ... and why?

Now that you understand the nature of children's sleeping and have had a look at the reasons why sleep problems happen, you might be able to see what kind of a sleep problem that your child has. Importantly, you probably have an inkling as to the reason or reasons why. If you've kept a sleep diary, it will have given you an honest and real view of their sleep overall, and may even have given you some more clues about where the sleep problem is coming from.

As we have already seen, there is always a reason why a child does not sleep well. In a healthy, typically developing child, a long-term sleep problem is most likely to be down to behavioural factors, but all toddlers and young children have occasional periods of poor sleep caused by bad dreams, illness, and so on.

Take a very honest look at what is happening around your child's sleep. You may have a fantastic bedtime routine; you may avoid having them watch too much TV before bed; you may keep a careful eye on their diet to make sure that they are not high on sugar; and so forth. There may be *just one tiny thing* going wrong for you (coming into bed with you for the last sleep cycle of the night? Stroking their back to get them to sleep at the start of the night? Lying beside their cot or bed when they wake during the night?). Unwittingly, one of those small factors may be causing the misery of your broken nights. It can be very hard, when you are a loving, sensible and diligent parent, to admit that there is something that you might be doing wrong around your child's sleep, but you need to look very carefully at all of your routines.

There is no doubt at all that some children are better sleepers than others. You might be the parent of more than one child and have never had problems with your other ones. Your bedtime routine with your sleepless child may be just the same as it was with the others, so why are you having a problem now? The fact is that all children are individual, and while, for example, falling asleep on your bed and then being transferred to their own will not cause later waking problems for some children, for others it is the reason behind night time waking and distress.

You are about to change the way that you approach bedtime practices with your child, but this does not mean that what you have been doing previously has been wrong. It is just that it is not sustainable right now, for any of you.

Setting your goal

Once you have established the exact nature of your child's sleep problem, it is very helpful to set goals as to what you want their sleep to be like. Sometimes when working with families, I ask the parents to describe their perfect bedtime scenario. Often, they are a little bit reluctant because they feel that what they would like – a happy bedtime routine followed by a kiss good night, their child to fall asleep alone and sleep through the night – is not possible. This impossible dream is actually reality for most families, and there is absolutely no reason why it shouldn't be for you, too!

Based on what you have learned so far about your child's sleep, you might find it helpful to get a notebook or a piece of paper and write down a clear summary of what is happening and why, along with what you would like to achieve. You can use the overview below as a guide.

An overview of my child's sleep

My child's typical night's sleep is like this:	They take a long time to fall asleep at the beginning of the night. They will not go into their own bed, and they need to fall asleep on my bed with me close by. When they are asleep, I carry them through to their own room and put them to bed while they are asleep. They wake up later, screaming. The only way to settle them is for them to come into my bed. They then sleep all night with me, but they wriggle and kick the covers off.

(*Continued*)

My child is not sleeping through the night because:	They can only fall asleep with me lying with them in my bed at the beginning of the night. This means that when they wake later, they get upset and need to come to my bed and have me to lie with them again.
What I want is for them to:	Be happy to fall asleep in their bed at bedtime and sleep through the night there.
To achieve this, I need to:	• Teach them how to go to sleep happily in their bed at the start of the night. • Help them to learn that their bed is a safe and permanent place to sleep. • Break the ritual of them getting into my bed during the night. • Praise them for independent sleeping.

Getting motivated

By now, hopefully you have established the exact nature of your child's sleep problem and you are clear about your goal and what you want for them. You should also have a strong idea about how you are going to achieve that goal. The trouble is, though, that you are already exhausted and you feel a bit demoralized, especially if you've tried to tackle their sleeping difficulties before.

In these circumstances, it can be very difficult to summon up the confidence and motivation needed for change. Take your notebook or piece of paper then try the following three exercises:

1. Name three good things that will arise from improving your child's sleep.
2. Name three things that you yourself have achieved over the past year.

3. Name three things that are holding you back from teaching your child to sleep through the night.

Example

The three good things that will come from my child sleeping better are:

1 They'll be better tempered during the day.
2 I'll be able to function better at work.
3 My partner and I will have more time for one another.

Three things that I have achieved over the past year are:

1 I've been promoted at work.
2 I've decorated the living room.
3 I've learned how to grow plants from seeds.

The things that are holding me back from teaching my child to sleep through the night are:

1 I'm scared of them crying. I don't believe that's right.
2 I like the contact with them during the night.
3 I'm worried that I might be too exhausted to carry it through.

Once you have been honest with yourself about what might be holding you back from teaching your child to sleep, you will be better placed to make a choice about whether you really want to undertake sleep training and, if so, which method to choose.

If you decide to postpone tackling your child's sleep, or if you plan to leave things as they are for the long term, then at least you can be sure in your own mind that you have made the decision and it is a positive choice.

This can be very helpful because, for many people, to feel that their child's behaviour is outside their control, or to have the vague sense that they ought to be addressing the sleep issue but haven't, can be more unsettling than the sleep problem itself.

If you have decided that you really do want to commence tackling the sleep problem, it's really good to start preparing to make the changes.

Taking care of practicalities ... and caring for yourself

Let's start with some simple forward planning:

1. If your child is currently sleeping in bed with you, take some time to adjust mentally to the fact that they will soon be sleeping in their own cot or bed. However positive you might feel about the move, you may find that you have a small sense of regret, too. Make the most of your last few nights together, and check out your feelings. It may be that you can't wait for them to sleep in their own bed, but equally, despite the fact that their sleep and your own are disrupted, you fear that you will miss having them with you. Remember that, even when they are sleeping in their own space, they can still be welcomed into your bed in the morning for a loving cuddle.

2. You will need to prepare any older (or younger) brothers and sisters for the changes that you plan to make. Even the gentlest approach will involve some degree of crying, and if siblings are not used to hearing this, they may worry. Reassure them that you are teaching their brother or sister how to sleep in their own bed/without having milk/without you lying on their bedroom floor, and so on. Tell them that when they hear their sibling cry, you are awake and dealing with them. If your other children are used to their sibling always being in your bed/making you tired/waking *them* up at night, they will possibly be glad that you are doing something about it.

   Siblings may be disturbed by more than just bedtime/night-time crying. When you introduce the changes, you might have to leave them to their own devices at the start of the night, as you deal with your little one who's having the problem sleeping. This is especially the case if your partner is at work or you're bringing up your family on your own. Once again, give as full an explanation as they can understand, and after you have managed to settle the little one who is struggling with their sleep, you can turn your attention to your other one(s). Thank them for waiting, and if your children are sharing a room, praise the other child for being patient and kind, or even for demonstrating to their brother or sister how to stay calmly in their bed. You can show them how much they are valued by rewarding their tolerance with a special treat, such as choosing their favourite meal for the family's dinner. Any sacrifices that they have made in terms of the loss of your attention or being disturbed during the night will be rewarded soon by having a parent with more energy and more time for them.

3. Similarly, if you have close neighbours, you should let them know that you are about to teach your toddler to sleep. They will appreciate the courtesy and are more likely to support you. Many times, sleep plans have had to be abandoned when parents fear disturbing or upsetting their neighbours. As with other children, if they are not used to hearing your child cry excessively at night, they may fear that something has happened to them or to you. If they understand the reason for the disruption, they are more likely to be able to tolerate it.

4. Choose a period of relative quiet and stability in which to start the new routine. You are more likely to be able to stick with it if things are calm at work, or if you don't have too many family or social demands. Although waiting for a quiet time might mean that you have to postpone changing your child's sleep habits, it is better that you start later and achieve success (although you should avoid putting it off indefinitely!). Even if just one of you is going to be largely responsible for implementing the changes, you should check out what your partner's schedule is going to be like and

choose a time when they are able to support you. For most people, commencing a sleep plan at the start of the weekend is an ideal time.

5. Both you and your partner being equally committed to the process of improving your child's sleep is so important. If one of you looks after the children and the other one goes out to paid work, you may worry that night-time disturbance might make work for your partner the next day extremely difficult. They might have a low tolerance of your child crying and they might even see it as your responsibility to get up and use any means to stop it, regardless of the long-term implications of this. If your partner is like this, it might be helpful to suggest that they sleep in another room, if that is possible, for a short period. You also need to help them see that helping your child to sleep will ultimately benefit all of you.

6. If you are in paid work, you should consider informing your manager and colleagues about what you are planning to do. They may not be able to decrease your workload, but they may be a little more understanding if you seem extra tired at work. Sharing information about home (especially if it is about children) can often lead to warmer working relationships. Over the few nights of sleep changes, you may value your colleagues' interest in how you are doing, as well as their advice and understanding.

7. Most important of all, you need to prepare yourself for the impact of the sleep changes. Get as much support lined up as you can from friends, family and work colleagues. Before you start, you need to get as much rest as you possibly can. Although evenings, after your child has gone to bed, may be the only time that you can catch up on admin or watch TV, you need to go to bed early for a few nights.

Things to remember

- It is never too late to help your child improve their sleep.
- Don't let fear of things getting worse put you off changing the way that they sleep – they often don't and, if they do, it will be temporary and leading to a positive end.
- Even if things do get a bit worse, you are in control now and you will feel more positive.
- Thoughtful preparation is one of the keys to successful sleep changes.
- Think honestly about the things that are causing your child's sleep problems. Being honest with yourself doesn't mean being hard on yourself.
- Don't blame yourself. You haven't got a sleep problem on your hands because you've been stupid, lazy or careless. Many sleep problems originate when parents are *extra* caring, selfless and attentive!
- Be clear about what you want to achieve when you are setting your goals.
- Don't even think about changing your child's sleep habits just because someone else has told you that you need to. If you're happy with the situation as it is, there is no need to change it.

Insight

The starting point of any sleep improvement is to help a child to fall asleep alone in their bed at the start of the night.

If a child already falls asleep by themselves at bedtime but is waking in the night looking for a familiar ritual, such as a bottle of milk to come into your bed, you need to change some of their usual cues and the way that they fall asleep at bedtime. This will engineer some protest, help to alter their expectations of what will happen later in the night, and, in a way, perform a reset.

Explaining to your child

Before you start making any kind of sleep changes with your toddler or child, you should *always* explain beforehand what is going to happening. It is good to respect your child's feelings, and letting them know what is going to happen and why shows them that you care about them. Besides, just to dramatically alter the way that they usually fall asleep with no prior warning or reason can be very alarming and frightening for them.

So, first of all, explain to your child in simple, age-appropriate and straightforward terms that they are going to (choose the one which applies or make up your own goal):

- sleep by themselves
- go to sleep *after* their bottle of milk instead of *with* it
- sleep in their bed instead of in yours.

Tell them that you are going to help them with this, and that you will still be very close by.

Avoid bargaining, negotiating or saying things like 'You'll be very tired tomorrow if you don't get a good night's sleep' or 'I am *so* tired, and I really need you to sleep tonight.' Your child doesn't have a sleep problem on purpose, and saying things like this can make them feel pressurized or guilty. Equally, offering rewards that they can't achieve on their own is unfair. Saying 'If you don't wake up tonight, we will go and get an ice cream' makes it tough for your child, who can't *help* waking up, first because they don't get the treat and second, because they feel like they've let you down.

Once you've explained what is going to happen, you need to follow a calm and familiar bedtime routine with (for children over two years old) an awake window of over five hours, so that they have had enough time awake to build up enough sleep pressure to enable them to fall asleep.

Insight

A lovely way to finish the bedtime routine is to ask your child what the best bit of their day was, and to share your best bit, too. The sharing of these 'golden moments' means that you say good night on a very positive note.

10

Taking control and helping your child to sleep well – the techniques

We've talked a lot about how important it is for your child to be able to settle alone at bedtime, and I know that, for many parents and children, this can be difficult. In the case studies I have illustrated some of the techniques that can be used to help a child learn how to self-settle, and in this chapter, for clarity, I describe them in more detail.

Techniques for helping a child to settle alone – a menu of options

Sleep changing techniques for toddlers broadly fall into two basic categories. These are:

1. **Controlled crying** – leaving your child to cry until they go to sleep alone, returning to reassure them briefly at specified intervals.
2. **Gradual withdrawal** – remaining with your child as they learn to settle to sleep in their own bed or cot, and then gradually moving away from them until they learn how to sleep alone.

Below are the versions and variations of these two techniques which I have developed and used with families over very many years, and which I know are both successful and emotionally safe.

With all these techniques the first aim is for your child to simply stay in their bed. They should be praised when they don't get out of bed or when they lie down if they are in a cot.

It will take them a long time to actually fall asleep at first, and this is not their fault. So, rather than telling them to go to sleep, you should instead tell them to stay in their bed/snuggle down/ get cosy and so on.

Quick Step Return

This is the starting point for most toddler and child sleep improving. More often than not, it is the only technique that is needed, and it will work within a week.

Suitable for:

- toddlers and children still in a cot
- children who will stay in their bed if you ask them to
- children with a safety gate in their doorway.

How to do it:

- Follow a calm, loving and consistent bedtime routine.
- At the end of it, tell your child that you are going to do some jobs and you'll be coming back and checking that they are cosy. (Don't say you're checking that they are OK – why *wouldn't* they be?)
- Return every two minutes or so to praise them for being alone and to *briefly* reassure them. Spend just a few seconds with them. The purpose of you going to them is to let them know that you are around and all is well. You are *not* going in to calm them down and settle them to sleep. They need to learn that bit for themselves – but knowing that you are nearby.
- If your child gets out of bed, take them back again and tell them that they must stay in their bed. If they won't get into bed, don't fight with them; just leave them at the gate and try again when you go back to them two minutes later.
- If they seem frightened or very upset, you need to remain calm. Tell them that you can see that they are frightened/

upset, and then tell them that they are OK/safe, that you are just outside their room, you can hear them and you will keep coming back.

- If they tell you that they are scared about monsters for example, you should once again, acknowledge their fear and then respond with something like 'The good thing is that monsters are pretend. They're only in books and films.'
- If they tell you that they are worried about something more realistic like burglars or murderers, you should listen, then reassure them that the house is secure and that the police/ Neighbourhood Watch/CCTV is keeping an eye on your area.
- Make sure that you go back every two minutes; your child needs to trust you. Praise them if they are in the bed/lying down and, if necessary, keep going back until they fall asleep during one of your absences.
- If they try to delay you by asking for more cuddles/stories/food or wanting to talk to you, you need to say kindly and firmly, 'We'll talk about that/do that/see to that in the morning', then leave with confidence and continue to go back several times, praising them if they are lying nicely in bed.
- Eventually, out of tiredness rather than choice, they will manage to go to sleep. When they do this, even though it wasn't really their decision to fall asleep, you should be very proud of them and of yourself, because taking that first step is such a positive move, and now you are on the right track to peaceful nights!

Quick Step Return will work for most children, but some just can't be safely left alone. If they refuse to stay in bed, start breaking or throwing things in their room, or take their clothes and nappy off, you can start off with Quick Step Return and then add in another technique that I call simply Standing Quietly.

Standing Quietly

Suitable for:

- toddlers and children who are no longer in a cot
- those that can't stay in their bed or room
- those who take off their clothes (including their nappy)
- those who throw things around the room and/or can't be safely left alone.

How to do it:

- Start off with Quick Step Return but, if your child is unable to stay in their bed or be contained by the stair gate in their doorway, you should go into their room and close the door behind you. Stand facing your child but with your back to the door. Have some soft, dim lighting in the room, for your child's reassurance and also so that you can see what you are doing.
- Give a direction just once – for example, 'Climb into your bed now,' then stand quietly, watch and wait until they move towards doing it. It will probably take some time for them to do as you ask, but try just waiting it out, standing very still and not over-repeating the instruction. You need to avoid saying things like 'Come on, I've asked you twice! You're going to be very tired if you don't go to bed! I'm tired, and I've got to be up early tomorrow!' Just keep calm, quiet and still. If you need to remind them, just say quietly, 'I'm waiting for you to get into your bed, my love.' If they try to procrastinate, delay or distract you with things like 'I want to sleep in your bed!' 'I'm hungry!' 'I love you!' and all the other things that will melt your heart and make you feel like the worst parent on the planet, just stay calm and don't engage in the conversation until they are back in bed. Then you can say, 'You can come into my bed for a cuddle in the morning!' 'You can have a lovely big breakfast in the morning!' 'I love you, too!'

- As soon as they start to move towards getting into bed, you can start the warm praise, saying something like 'I'm so proud of you for getting into bed!'
- You would then, after responding *briefly* to their requests or concerns, give them a loving cuddle and carry on with Quick Step Return.

You may have to repeat Standing Quietly a few times before your child eventually settles to sleep without you in the room. However, give them time and remember that biology is on your, and their, side. They will eventually fall asleep.

Case study
Two-and-a-half-year-old boy, Felix, who would take off his pyjamas and nappy and wee on the floor if his parents left him to fall asleep alone.

The situation
Felix was described by his parents as a gentle and mild boy. He was healthy and developing well. He had recently become a big brother to Layla, who was 12 weeks old when I met the family.

Before Layla was born, Felix had no problems sleeping without either of his parents in the room with him. Now he wanted his mum to sit on the sofa in his room until he went to sleep, and, if she didn't, he would take his nappy off and wet the bedroom floor. His mum would wash his feet and bring a cloth and bucket of water to wash the carpet, then try to put him back to bed. He would do this repeatedly when she tried to leave and would sometimes still be awake after 9.30 p.m. if she wasn't beside him.

He had a great bedtime routine with lots of repetition and consistency. He had recently had his cot converted to a bed after having climbed out of it, and he had a stair gate in his bedroom doorway. Felix had dropped his daytime nap early, just before his second birthday, and so when it was approaching 7 p.m., he was very tired.

Once he was asleep, he tended to sleep through the night, and he had a sleep training clock which was set for 6.45 a.m. to let him know when it was morning.

The solution

The fact that Felix had recently had a baby sister and was looking for some reassurance was not lost on his parents. They needed to find a way to help him regain his good sleep habits without making him feel pushed away or undervalued. They also needed to find a way of establishing a loving and practical routine which could be used for both children together and did not involve Mum going to a separate room for a long period at bedtime to settle baby Layla.

The sleep plan

- When Layla has her final nap, have a few minutes of precious 'you and me' time with Felix, spent cuddling/reading or just chatting together before starting the bedtime routine.
- Bath the children together, and afterwards, all three of you go to Felix's room to get dressed for the night.
- Then sit on Felix's bed, and both children have their milk as you chat to Felix and read some books.
- After this, you and Felix together can take Layla to her cot and put her down to settle to sleep. If she is a little unsettled, you will soon be going back to her.
- Then take Felix to the toilet for one last wee and put his nappy on.
- Tuck him into bed, kiss him good night, and then tell him that you are going to do some jobs and will be back soon to check on him. Leave the room with confidence and have his door a bit open and the safety gate fastened.
- He should have some water in a little beaker within easy reach.
- Go and check that Layla is OK, and then return to Felix within a minute or two (without Layla in your arms), and praise him warmly if he has stayed in his bed.
- Leave again, and return to him every few minutes until he is either lying quietly in his bed or asleep.
- **If he calls out for you**, tell him that you'll be there in a minute. When you go to him, praise him and give him a brief kiss.
- **If he gets out of bed**, you should greet him at the gate and tell him that he needs to go back to bed. Take him back to bed in silence and stay with him for a just a few moments to tell him that he needs to stay in bed. Don't tell him that you have to go and attend to Layla. Don't tell him that he's waking Layla up either.
- If he asks for anything, the only things that you can concede is having a drink of water or going to the toilet.

- If he takes his nappy off and wets the floor, stay in the room with him and close the door behind you. Pick up his nappy or get a new one if it is wet, and ask him to come to you so that you can put it back on. Stand and wait quietly until he does this. It may take some time, but you need to wait it out. When he does come to you, you should thank him and give him a little cuddle. Then quickly put the nappy back on for him and put him back to bed. Don't wash his feet as you usually do or mop up the carpet. Urine has no germs in it and it will do no harm to his health if he goes to bed with a little wee on his feet for a few nights. You can wash his feet and the carpet in the morning.
- Once he's back in the bed, give him a quick cuddle and then leave the room but reassure him that you're coming back.
- Eventually, he will run out of steam and when this happens you should not be in the room with him. If he falls asleep on his bedroom floor, pick him up and settle him in his bed.
- If Felix wakes during the night and calls for you, you need to go to him and, if necessary, take him back to bed and explain gently that it is still time for sleep. Tell him that he's woken up too soon.
- Go back to him every few minutes as you did at the beginning of the night. If he doesn't go back to sleep, just get him up any time after 6.45 a.m. Before you do this, you will need to open his curtains and remark that the sun is up on his clock!
- Once you've opened his curtains, you can welcome him to the day. Find some aspect of his sleeping that has been good and immediately praise him: 'You went to sleep all by yourself!' Reinforce the praise with a piece of pasta to collect in a jar. When his jar is full he can cook the pasta or have a special treat.

The outcome

As soon as Felix's parents had a plan, they felt better. On the first night it took an hour and 15 minutes for him to fall asleep alone. He took his nappy off just once and wet the floor, but his mum stayed calm and he quickly gave her the dry nappy to put back on. He didn't remove his nappy again after that. It took about ten nights for him to get fully back to his usual sleeping habits. He would have a run of good nights and then a couple of difficult nights. This is absolutely normal: with children, sleep progress is not always linear – you can expect the odd blip. At the start of the process he tended to settle better for his dad than his mum, and, once again, this is normal. Very often, children will settle more easily for one parent than the other. In Felix's case, he was expecting a softer response from his mum. When he figured out that both parents' response was the same, he began to settle to sleep at bedtime more easily and feeling less upset. It also helped that his baby sister was introduced into *his* bedtime routine and wasn't the main focus of his parents' (especially his mum's) attention.

Conclusion

Felix was taking his nappy off and wetting the floor so that his parents wouldn't leave him at bedtime. The arrival of his sister meant that sometimes his mum was busy with her at bedtime and not able to give Felix the time and attention that he was used to.

Now that Layla was three months old, she was ready to have a bedtime routine of her own, so luck would have it that the parents got in touch with me at the perfect time.

By combining the children's bedtime routine, giving Felix more time, and dealing with his nappy removal in a calm and sensible way, the problem was soon overcome. Just because an approach to solving a child's sleep problems is about changing their behaviour; it does not mean that their feelings are ignored.

Closing the Door

Many parents who have a toddler or a young child who won't stay in their bed have resorted to closing and holding their child's bedroom door. Often, it is done in anger or exasperation, and afterwards, the child has been very upset and the parent has felt awful about having done it. Usually, the door closing is the final part of a tense and unhappy bedtime routine, after which the child agrees to go sleep and the parent agrees to sit beside them. This is not a good situation, as the child might feel upset and confused and the parent may feel resentful and out of control.

Closing the door on your child is rather like using a 'controlled crying' technique with a baby in a cot. It is quite a serious move, and I wouldn't recommend it as the best way to help a child to sleep alone. However, I know that there are times when parents feel so out of control that they will close their child's bedroom door. If you're going to do it, you need to do it safely and to make sure that it is going to have a very swift and positive outcome. That outcome needs to be that your child will learn how to fall asleep alone and while feeling safe.

Suitable for:

- toddlers and children no longer in a cot
- those that can't stay in their bed and don't have a stair gate in their room doorway
- children who are not fearful about being left alone.

How to do it:

- Once again, start off with Quick Step Return, but if your child keeps getting up after a lengthy period and after you have asked them to stay in their bed, and if you are sure that they are not genuinely afraid or unwell, you can calmly tell them, if they get up again/won't return to bed, you will close the door for a minute.
- Don't keep threatening it, which will cause them to feel uncertain. Be prepared to carry it through as soon as your child gets up again or won't go back to bed.
- Make sure there's some light on in the room and then leave the room and close the door behind you, holding it if you need to. It's OK to speak quietly from the other side of the door, but wait for one minute (no longer) and then carefully open the door and go back in to them.
- Take them back to bed if necessary, and then praise them once they are in it. Tell them that, if they stay in bed, you will leave the door open and you will keep coming back every couple of minutes to check on them.
- Don't let their 'reward' for staying in their bed be having you sit beside them, as this is confusing and defeats the object. You can and should, however, keep going back to them if they are wide awake and praising them for staying in their bed.
- You might need to close the door quite a few times at first, and each time you do, you need to be calm, quiet and strong.

As you can see, Standing Quietly and/or Closing the Door are techniques that you only need to use as an addition to Quick Step Return if your child cannot stay in their bed or in their room.

Gradual Withdrawal

Suitable for:

- toddlers and children who are currently being rocked or fed to sleep
- those who usually fall asleep in your bed/on the sofa/anywhere that isn't their own bed
- some toddlers and children with medical or developmental difficulties
- parents who want a very gentle approach.

How to do it:
If your child is still in a cot:

- Make sure that their cot base is at its lowest setting, so that they can't climb out.
- If the cot is in your room, place it at a distance from your bed. The foot of your bed is ideal if there is space there. Otherwise, if your child has a room of their own, start the gradual withdrawal process in there from the first night.
- Explain to them that they are going to sleep in their cot and you're going to help them.
- Follow a consistent bedtime routine, with the loving finish, talking about their 'golden moments' if they are old enough or able to.
- Put them into the cot, and if they are not upset about it, just potter about, coming in and out of the room. If and when they do start to cry, go and kneel down right beside the cot and embrace them as they stand up, but don't get them out of the cot.

- If they are standing and you are kneeling, then you should both be roughly at the same level and you will be able to put your cheek next to theirs and cuddle them, albeit with the cot side between you both.
- Lay them down every few minutes if you can, and if this feels like a fight or a tussle, then just hold them until they eventually start to tire and then you can guide them safely down into a sleeping position.
- Stay with them until they are asleep.
- When they wake in the night or very early in the morning (which they are very likely to do, owing to you being beside them as they fell asleep), you should go back to them and kneel down, holding them as you did when they originally fell asleep.
- Don't expect or try to make them go back to sleep by themselves when they wake up in the night. It will be too difficult and confusing for them.
- **Don't go through any night-time or dawn rituals such as giving a feed, bringing them to sleep in your bed, letting them play a video game, and so on.**
- Throughout this whole settling process, both at bedtime and also during the night, you can and should give as much eye contact and physical contact as they need to settle, so long as they remain in their cot.
- After two or three nights, once your child becomes comfortable about falling asleep in the cot, it is time to withdraw some of your physical contact. However don't leave them alone yet. Instead, remain beside the cot and reduce your contact slightly. As they fall asleep, try patting the mattress instead of patting your child.
- After another two or three nights, you can sit at a little distance from the cot. Try doing a little bit of yoga breathing, or you could read a book if you have an eBook reader. If they cry, go back to them and reassure them briefly before moving away again.

- Repeat this, moving your chair a little further away from your child's cot each night until you are outside the room. Do this in tiny stages, so that they have time to get used to the change.

If your child

- The same principles apply as above – so follow a consistent bedtime routine, at the right time, and explain that they are going to sleep in their bed.
- Sit beside their bed but not in it or on it.
- Don't lie on the floor and pretend to go to sleep. If you do this, it is a bit misleading for them and they might feel let down when they wake later and you're not there (unless you've genuinely fallen asleep and you're there for the night!).
- Stay beside them until they go to sleep.
- If they won't stay in their bed, if they want to sit on your knee, or play with their toys, you can keep them 'on task' by using the Standing Quietly technique.
- Get up from your position beside their bed and stand facing them, with your back to their closed bedroom door. Tell them once to go back to bed or stop playing with their toys. Then wait it out quietly until they make a move to do as you have asked, at which point praise them warmly and go and sit beside them again.
- If they simply want to chat to you or cuddle you, as lovely as that is, you need to tell them that you can chat or have nice big cuddles in the morning.
- With any of these techniques, the two concessions that you would make would be if your child asks to go to the toilet or to have a drink of water.

In this book I want to give you as much information as possible, so that you can make an informed choice about how to handle your child's sleep problem. However, when you have a two- or three-year-old child and you're gradually inching your way out of the bedroom, I feel that, unless you really can't bear to do the Quick Step Return, the gradu~~al~~ ~~~~ ~~~~an seem a bit tentative and at odds with th~~~~ ~~~~meanour that I recommend because I know that ~~~~d so well to it.

A hybrid technique

If the thought of leaving your child to settle alone is too daunting but the thought of sitting beside them doesn't appeal or hasn't worked for you, then you might like to try this sensible and pragmatic approach that I've used very successfully with many families.

- Put your child into their bed or cot after a consistent bedtime routine with a loving finish.
- Leave the room for 2 minutes and then come back and sit beside them until they go to sleep.
- On the second night, leave for 2 minutes, come back and stay for 2 minutes and then leave for 2 minutes for a second time before coming back and sitting with them until they go to sleep.
- Over the coming nights, increase the number of your exits and returns by one each night. This will get your child used to the idea of you leaving and trusting that you will come back. It will manage any sense of anxiety that they might have about you going.

Of course, the risk is that it may prolong the time that it takes for them to fall asleep, and they may at first resist going to sleep until you come back. As we know, however, sleep will inevitably happen at some point, and the chances are that when you've done 20 or more 'exits and returns', your child is unlikely to resist eventually falling asleep – without you in the room.

This technique takes time and a lot of patience on your part, but if you're uncomfortable with the other methods, it is worth giving this a go.

When they wake in the night

As I've mentioned many times, it is normal for children to wake in the night with the sleep cycles, and as morning approaches, their sleep becomes especially light as their cortisol levels rise in preparation for the day. When your child wakes in the night, there is no need to presume that something is the matter. If they call for you or come to find you, don't ask them what is wrong, but instead tell them that they've woken up a bit too soon and now it's time to go back to sleep. Of course, if they *tell you* that they feel scared or sick or need a drink, then you will respond to what they need.

Provided everything is all right and your child has just woken naturally, you need to help them fall asleep as they did at the start of the night. Depending on which technique you are using, this will be either without having you in the room with them, or with you sitting beside (but not in) their bed. You may have to go through the whole process of popping in and out of the room, sitting beside the bed, standing quietly or even closing the door for a minute again if that's what you did at the start of the night. Remember that this is a temporary situation and that, even though it is very tough being woken in the night, if you can stay strong and consistent, your broken nights will soon be just a memory.

Insight

So many attempts at sleep training go wrong because it is only the start of the night that gets addressed. The start of the night is important, of course, but you will get nowhere with improving your child's sleeping if you then continue with night feeds or bringing them into bed with you during the night.

When they get up in the morning

With any learning experience but especially one that involves you separating from your child at bedtime, rewards in the morning are incredibly important. Giving warm praise for what they have achieved will make them as well as you feel good. It will emphasize that, despite you not staying with them as they fell asleep, you still love them the same as always. It will help their new, independent sleep behaviour to stick, too.

When you praise your child for good sleeping, you need to be very clear and let them know precisely what they've done well. It's good to praise them for general 'good sleeping', of course, but it is even better to be specific and say, 'You went back to bed when I asked you to!' or 'You waited in your bed for me to come back!' or 'You went to sleep all by yourself!'

If you would like to, you can back the praise up with a tangible reward like a sticker to put on their pyjamas. As you'll have noticed from the case studies, with children over the age of two, I often advise parents to get a clean, empty jam jar into which, each time their child achieves the goal of sleeping alone, they put a piece of dried pasta. When the jar is full, they can either cook the pasta with you, or have a treat, such as a special outing or a toy.

If you are going to use rewards, they work best when only mentioned at the time that they are given – for example, in the morning. At bedtime or during the night, saying, 'If you go back to bed now, you can have pasta for your jar in the morning' will not be enough of an incentive to tempt your child into their bed. And if they are upset and crying, it might even annoy and upset them more. It is much better to wait until they have achieved success and then reward them: 'Let's put a piece of pasta into your jar, because you went to sleep by yourself last night!' Of course, whether your child achieves the reward is down to you. If you are confident, resolute, and able to stand firm, then they can't help but succeed.

It's important to reward them even if they did not sleep alone out of choice. At first, when you help your child to change the way that they sleep, they will fall asleep only because they have run out of steam and have no more energy to stay awake. It is likely to take an hour or even longer for this to happen on the first few nights. Your aim during this time is just to change their sleep behaviour, and to do so in a calm and responsive way. This means checking in with them very regularly and giving encouragement, reassurance and praise, but not staying with them. Once they have changed their sleep or bedtime behaviour, the happy *feelings* will follow on. So, even though the first few nights of independent sleeping will involve tears and your child won't fall into a happy sleep, it won't always be like this. Typically, within a week or so (every child is different), your child will be falling asleep quickly and happily after the new routine.

Making a plan and sticking with it

Hopefully, by now you should have an idea of the reason or reasons behind your child's sleeping problems. You should also now know about the techniques that you can use to help them, and you've decided on a time when you're able to start. You've also let people know what you're going to be doing, so now it is time for you to make a plan!

It's fine to just have things clear in your head, but some people work better with something written down so get your notebook out again or grab your piece of paper! Writing your plan will give it clarity and help to focus your thoughts. Remember that simple is best. You might like to design your own sleep plan or try something like the sleep action plan below.

My child is not sleeping well because:	The solution is:	The obstacles are:	The way that I will deal with this is:
She is scared of monsters and she needs me to be next to her as she sleeps.	I will acknowledge her fear and also keep letting her know that monsters are pretend.	I can't bear to see her upset or think of her being afraid.	I will drop or limit her nap, so that she is more tired and less anxious at bed time. Then I'll do the Quick Step Return technique with lots of reassurance.
She then wakes in the night upset and I have to sleep next to her again.	I will help her learn how to fall asleep alone in her bed.	My partner expects me to keep her quiet in the night.	I will ask them for their support and explaining the benefits. If they won't help me, I'll get them earplugs or let them sleep elsewhere until things are better
He can only fall asleep when he is given a bottle of milk in his cot.	Teach him some new sleep associations and remove the feed/sleep association that he has developed.	He loves his milk and I don't want to take away something that he enjoys so much.	I will give him his milk, sitting on my knee, and read a story before he goes into his cot. If he is upset and unable to sleep without the bottle, I will stay with him and use the **Gradual withdrawal technique.**
This means that he wakes in the night looking for more milk, and he doesn't eat well in the day.	Drop his night feeds and let his body rest and repair	My family says that the milk is good for him and will help him sleep better.	I will explain that milk is a nutritious drink but he's having too much of it, and it is causing him to wake rather than helping him to sleep.

She seems to be "programmed" to wake at 4 am!	Control her cortisol levels that are responsible for her early waking.	I feel a bit out of control with managing her sleep.	I will re establish her lunch time nap and put her to bed a bit earlier so that she's not so over tired.
	Stop the ritual of her getting into my bed at 4 am.	I'm just so tired, I can't help it!	I will go to bed as early as possible and be mentally prepared to be up with her at 4 am, encouraging her to stay in her bed and giving her as long as it takes. I will explain to her at bed time that she is going to stay in her own bed until "proper morning." I will get a sleep training clock to help her understand when it's morning and establishing some rewards for staying in her bed.
Stop the morning nap which prevents her from having an afternoon nap and then leaves her over tired at bed time.		It's impossible to keep her awake around 9 am when she is tired.	If necessary I will let her have a cat nap of 20 minutes at 9 am and then gently wake her and put her in her cot for a nap just after her lunch.

Making it work

Once you have made a plan to start changing your child's sleep habits, you need to demonstrate the three Cs:

- consistency
- calmness
- confidence.

These three qualities will make the process easier for both you and them. There may be times when your resolve weakens, and you need to be prepared for these.

If you possibly can, you should seek out someone to support you during this process. Practical help, such as someone taking your child or children off your hands for a couple of hours during the day to allow you to catch up on some rest, is absolutely invaluable and will keep you going. If you have been up in the middle of the night, things will not look so bleak if you know that you will get a two-hour nap the following day.

Sometimes, all you need is some moral support: someone telling you that you are doing a good job, encouraging and listening to you.

Stumbling blocks

Even if you've got a brilliant plan in place and are resolved and confident, you may still encounter some unexpected difficulties along the way. Here are some of the most common ones:

The problem	The solution
When my child cries, they sometimes vomit.	• Be as calm as possible, as you very quickly change the bedding. Do not bath them, but bring a warm flannel and just wipe their hands, face and hair if necessary. • Offer a small drink of water – but *not* a snack or a milk feed. • Keep the bedroom lights down low. • As soon as you have changed them and wiped up in the room, place them back into the cot or put them back to bed. • Speak kindly and reassure them but try not to reinforce the vomiting by stopping the sleep changing. If you do this, you may unwittingly encourage being sick as a habitual response to them being asked to do something that they don't want to. • Remember that toddlers have a very fragile gag reflex and the vomiting is more of a mechanical than emotional response (even though they are crying). It is not a sign of illness either.
They wake up their siblings when they cry.	• Explain to the other children in the family (if they are old enough to understand) that X is learning how to sleep at night and is feeling 'cross'. • Reassure them that you are awake and looking after them. • If it is a younger child or a baby that is being woken up, you will need to go between both of them in turn, offering reassurance that you're there. This difficult situation is temporary, and if you can hang on in there, it will soon be resolved. • Siblings are less likely to be woken up pre-midnight, when they are in deeper sleep. • Be aware that the disruption to other family members' sleep is short term and that, if you stick with the training, *all* of you will benefit.

(Continued)

The problem	The solution
They are crying more and for longer than I expected.	• Don't be frightened of the crying. • As long as you are close beside them or returning to them frequently and calmly, they will know that they have not been abandoned. • They are crying out of frustration at the change in their usual routine. • At bedtime, even if they are crying a lot, they will not cry all night. Sleep will eventually overtake them and they will sleep. • Try not to be upset if they don't fall into a happy sleep at first. The happy feelings will follow, once they have learned (however reluctantly) to fall asleep by themselves.
During the sleep training they catch a cold, have an injury during the day, or suffer a bout of teething.	• If they have pain, give a painkiller 20 minutes before bed and settle them still as per the plan. • If they wake in the night and are clearly uncomfortable or have a high temperature, you should get them out of the cot or bed and give some paracetamol/acetaminophen, a drink of water and a cuddle. • Hold them in your arms until they are calm and settled then try putting them back into the cot or bed and soothing them there. • If they continue to cry severely and you suspect that they are still feeling poorly, then continue to hold/rock them until they go to sleep. • If they have a temperature above 38 °C (100.4 °F) a rash or a different cry, you should get medical advice. • It's best not to go back to your old way of settling them, such as giving milk or bringing them into your bed or you may end up slipping backwards and needing to restart with the sleep changes.

The problem	The solution
We go on holiday, and it all goes to pot!	• As soon as you realize that your child's sleep has regressed, and it's not just jet lag/adjusting to the change, you need to get back on track rather than letting things slip further. • Introduce a new bedtime book or other element of change, such as a cup instead of a bottle for their bedtime drink. This will help you to do a reset. • In the light of the minor change at the start of the night, which will break the usual pattern and alter their expectations of your response to them as they settle to sleep or when they wake up, you can then restart the sleep training. • You can expect more resistance the second time around, but if you keep your cool and stay resolved and calm, it will work for you all again.

How long will it take?

When you make big changes to the way that your child sleeps, you can expect things to be a little bit worse for a few nights before they begin to improve. You should see an improvement, however, within a week. If you plan for the worst, it will be easier to cope when things are difficult. However, for many families, things can improve from the very first night. Certainly, when you as a parent feel confident, empowered and certain that you're doing the right thing, the whole sleep thing will feel less tentative or explosive.

It is a sensible precaution to avoid planning any special events when you know that you are going to be doing some sleep work.

You might want to plan ahead with food and stock up the freezer and cupboards with easy meals for the family, a week or so before you begin. Knowing that dinner times are sorted will give you more headspace to concentrate on your child's sleep.

It might be possible for you and/or your partner to take a day or two off work, so that you can support one another. Still send your child to their usual day-care provider ... and don't feel guilty about spending that time resting.

If you are at home full time and your child isn't in day care, try not to spend all day in the house alone together. Even though you are tired, it will do you both good to go out for a walk or to an organized activity at least once a day.

Evaluating your progress and keeping going

Once you have started to make changes to the way that your child sleeps, it is really good to evaluate your progress as you go. If you've had a difficult night, or if things seem to be dragging on, it is very useful to check out how far you have come and what you are still aiming for. Progress isn't always linear when it comes to toddlers' and children's sleeping, and it's not unusual to have good and bad nights at first. Taking a few moments in the morning to take an honest look at the night before will show you what improvements you have made and help you to keep motivated. It will also help you identify what, if anything, might be going wrong.

Every morning ask yourself the following questions:

1. What was good about their sleep last night?
2. What was bad about their sleep last night?
3. How far did I stick to the sleep plan?
4. Is there anything I could have done differently?
5. What am I going to do tonight?
6. Is there anything that I need to sort out to help me see this through?

Example

1 What was good about their sleep last night?
   They went to sleep in their own bed without having me in the room with them.
2 What was bad about their sleep last night?
   They woke up at 2 a.m. and took an hour to resettle. Normally, they would have gone straight back to sleep if I'd brought them into bed with me.
3 How far did I stick to the sleep plan?
   I stuck to it completely!
4 Is there anything I could have done differently?
   I could have left their bedroom door slightly open all night, as they were upset when they woke in the night and it was closed.
5 What am I going to do tonight?
   I am going to continue to teach them that their bed is a safe place and they can sleep there alone. The more I reinforce this, the easier it will become for them to fall asleep alone and resettle without me when they wake in the night. I'm also going to make sure that their environment is the same when they wake in the night as it was when they fell asleep.
6 Is there anything that I need to sort out to help me see this through?
   During this process I will have my dinner at the same time as my child, so that I can focus on them without being niggled by hunger.

When you evaluate your progress, you will need to keep your original goal in the forefront of your mind. Remind yourself of the advantages of what their good sleep will bring, not only for them, but for you and the rest of the family, too.

What if your sleep plan doesn't work?

You might have started a sleep plan with utter resolve and confidence. Your goals may have been clear and your plan utterly watertight, but somehow your child just didn't respond as you had hoped and you are left exhausted and asking yourself, 'Where did I go wrong?'

If your plan has not worked/is not working for you, it is down to one or more of the following reasons:

The method doesn't suit your natural, instinctive parenting style and/or your values

This means that your heart isn't really in it, and you need to consider the following:

- whether to try a different, gentler or firmer approach
- whether a part of you enjoys and allows contact with your child at bedtime during the night – if so, that's OK. Give yourself permission to enjoy the closeness! You should never feel under pressure from others to make changes that you feel are unnecessary.

You have got frustrated that the sleep training isn't working fast enough

If you've been doing a Gradual Withdrawal method and haven't seen an improvement, you might want to consider speeding up the process by moving on to Quick Step Return. Because you have already done some groundwork such as establishing a consistent bedtime routine and teaching them how to go to sleep, for example, in their bed rather than in your bed, this method will be less traumatic than if you had started it from scratch. It should be quicker, too.

Your child has been too upset by the process of sleep training

You should not give up and waste all of the efforts that you've both made, but rather switch to a gentler method. 'OK, I can't leave them alone to cry, but I can at least teach them how to go to sleep in their own bed.' Remaining close beside them as they make changes to their sleep behaviour and then withdrawing in small gradual stages will work better for you.

Outside factors such as an illness, holiday or house move have broken the consistency that is needed for success

These events of family life are usually outside of our control and can have a real impact on our children's sleep. The best that you can do is to put sleep training 'on ice' and try not to lose any ground that you might have gained. For instance, if you have been making progress and your child gets a bad cold, there is no reason to bring them into your bed again. It is better to comfort them in their room, with a cuddle, a drink of water and a dose of infant painkiller. Once they are calm and comfortable, you should resettle them in their bed, and if they are still poorly, make up a temporary bed for yourself on their floor if there is space. This kind of approach will give them the attention and contact that they need when they are unwell, while not allowing things to slip too far backwards.

Friends and family have questioned and criticized what you're doing

While up to a point it is good to listen to others' advice and to appreciate their concern for you and your child, it is ultimately your choice as their parent to care for them as you see fit. You know your own child better than anyone else and you also know your own limitations and capabilities. Acknowledge their concern, and tell them that your child's needs are your top priority. Of course, this is particularly difficult if the criticism is coming from your partner. If this is the case, you need to take the time to discuss what approach will not only benefit your child but also be acceptable to both of you.

You have not followed the method to its conclusion

It is not at all uncommon to make some changes, achieve a degree of success and then get stuck. If you are following a gradual withdrawal method, you need to see it to its conclusion, and not end up permanently sitting in the doorway as your child goes to sleep. Also, consistency is vital, and you need to make sure that your response to your child's night waking or dawn waking is *exactly* the same as your response when you originally put them to bed.

You have started following the sleep plan at the first or subsequent waking rather than at the beginning of the night

It is essential that, when you decide to implement your sleep plan, you concentrate first and foremost on how your child settles at the *beginning* of the night. I need to stress again that, if you allow your child, for example, to fall asleep downstairs on the sofa or in your bed, only to later transfer them to their bed or cot, they will naturally wake up later feeling alarmed. They will need you to recreate the circumstances under which they originally fell asleep at the start of the night, and now, having had the equivalent of a 'power nap', they will find it especially difficult to fall asleep again without your help. Try to capitalize on the fact that at the very start of the night they have a build-up of sleep pressure, melatonin and are surrounded by night-time sleep cues.

If you are failing to make progress and you need to switch techniques, it is worth also going back to the start of Chapter 9 and look at the list of reasons for toddlers and children's night waking. Is there anything there that you might have missed? Remember that 'sleep changing' at the start of the night will not work alone if there are other factors causing the night waking that need to be addressed.

You have done the sleep changing at the start of the night only

Your child needs your response to be consistent throughout the night. So, if you teach them, for example, to fall asleep in their bed rather than yours at the start of the night, and keep them in their own bed each time they wake in the night but then change tack at 5 a.m. (because in your head it is morning) and bring them into bed to sleep with you, you will hamper the learning process.

Ten sleep tips

1 It is important to choose a sleep changing method that matches your parenting style.
2 No matter how gentle a solution you choose, you should be prepared for your child to cry.
3 Despite the number of books on child sleep available, there are just two training methods.
4 Understanding *why* your child is waking and crying is the key to effective and gentle sleep training.
5 Writing down your goals and sleep plan will give you focus and clarity.
6 When you start making changes, your child needs you to be calm, confident and consistent.
7 Be prepared for things to go wrong, and try not to be discouraged if they do.
8 Accept that, when your child's sleep improves, it's down to your intervention – not coincidence.
9 If things are not progressing, you need to make a confident decision – whether to give it longer or change your approach.
10 Be honest with yourself when it comes to evaluating your progress.

Managing your own sleep needs

Many parents are shocked to find that, after helping their children to sleep through the night, they have somehow lost the ability to sleep themselves.

Being sleep deprived as an adult makes it really difficult to look after your family, go to work, love your partner and function as your normal self generally. Sleep deprivation makes us unwell and unhappy and can be dangerous. When adults are very low on sleep, we can experience several micro sleeps in the day. These can last for a few seconds, and we might not even be aware of them. It's important to know this, as these lapses can make it unsafe to drive, for example. In fact, recent research has shown that sleep deprivation causes impairment to cognitive functioning equivalent to 0.1 per cent alcohol in the blood. This is over the UK legal driving limit.

It is not surprising that, after several weeks, months or even years of deeply disturbed sleep, it can be difficult to regain a good sleep pattern. If you cast your mind back to how the sleep cycles work, you will recall that children tend to wake up as they are coming into a light sleep phase. Their waking is natural and therefore not too damaging. You, on the other hand, may have been used to being woken during the deep phase of your own sleep cycle, and after a time this disturbance can be very debilitating. You may have responded by not allowing yourself to relax fully into sleep, knowing that you are soon going to be woken up ... and so you now have a sleep problem. Don't worry. If you were a good sleeper before you had children, there is every chance that you can be a good sleeper again.

Start a relaxing, repetitive bedtime routine for yourself. Seriously, you will benefit from the sleep cues just as much as your child has!

- Turn screens off, and have one final look at your phone, before switching it on to silent mode, half an hour before you intend to get into bed.
- Go to bed at a reasonable time – that is, try not to let yourself become overtired, as this might mean that you struggle to switch off and go to sleep. Just the same as with your child,

the stress hormones produced when you are overtired will fight your natural sleep hormones.

- Go to bed and get up in the morning at roughly the same times. Keeping a consistent sleep/wake schedule will help programme your body to sleep.
- If you've a tendency to struggle to go to sleep at night, it's a good idea to avoid caffeine-containing drinks in the afternoon and evening.
- Avoid alcohol, too, as this interferes with the quality of your sleep. It might help you to get off to sleep, but it often causes night waking.
- If you can't relax and go to sleep, see if you can read a book. You may not be asleep, but your body will still be resting.
- If, when you turn off the light, you struggle to go to sleep, try the following mental exercise:

   Close your eyes and make an alphabetical list of, for instance, countries, birds or parts of the body, authors, singers or similar. This might sound silly, but this mental exercise prevents your mind from wandering, excessive planning or worrying. It can provide a focus and yet it is sufficiently unimportant as to not prevent you from sleeping. If you do this kind of exercise regularly, it can begin to act as a sleep prompt for you.

- If you do have something that is on your mind, allow yourself 15 minutes of planning or 'worry time'. This is all you need as, after that, your thoughts will just be going around in circles. After the 15 minutes, you should either get back to making your lists or get up, have a warm drink and then return to bed once you are feeling tired.
- If your partner snores, it won't help you to regain your healthy sleep habits. Ear plugs are not an option, as you need to be able to hear your child or children, and so you might therefore have to consider sleeping separately – at least until your sleep habits are re-established.

Once you know that your child's sleep problems are completely resolved, you will be better able to relax and fall back into your previous good sleep patterns.

Acknowledging and enjoying your achievement

Teaching your toddler or child how to improve their sleep is not easy, and it does sometimes require you to act against your instinct. It can be a very emotionally taxing experience that can make you question whether you are really doing the right thing.

But once you've done it, you will *know* that it was the right thing for all of you. Sleep is not an optional extra. It is *essential for life*, and without it we just can't function properly. By helping your child (and therefore yourself) to sleep, you have achieved something incredibly important, significant and *wonderful*!

To finish, I just want to remind you of the following things:

- You have seen that your child has a sleep problem and cared enough to want to help them.
- You have observed your child and assessed their sleep problem in a way that only you could have done.
- You have read and considered the advice and therefore given yourself the tools to help them.
- You have taken all that you've learned, and designed a strategy or sleep plan for your child.
- You have put that plan into practice – even though it might have been easier to give in at times.
- You have shown patience, resolve and compassion when your child and you were finding it tough going.
- You have allowed them to learn independent sleep skills, even when you have wanted to run to them and cuddle them to sleep or bring them into your bed!

- You have taken control and improved your own confidence as a parent.
- You have taught your child a vital life skill: the ability to enjoy sleep and all its benefits.
- You have improved their health, concentration and happiness.
- You have given them a precious gift – the gift of sleep.
- You should be *very* proud of yourself.

Index

acetaminophen, junior 134, 135
acknowledging/enjoying your achievement 190–191
additional needs 120
  ADHD 126–128
  autism ix, 120–126, 133
  cerebral palsy (CP) 128–129
  Down's syndrome 130–132, 133
  neuromuscular difficulties 128–129
ADHD (attention deficit and hyperactivity disorder) 126
  symptoms 126–127
  top ten tips 127–128
adopted children 113–118
adrenaline 7, 14, 75
allergies 17, 120, 132, 139
ambience 18–19
anaemia 48–49
anxiety 20, 25–35, 65, 68
arousals 4, 68, 70–71
asthma 68, 133, 138–139
atopic eczema 139–140
autism ix, 120–126, 133
awake windows 7

babysitting 110, 119
baths 37
bedroom light 11
beds 17, 82–85
bedtime fears 25–26, 65
  case study 30–35
  dos and don'ts 27–30
  separation anxiety 20, 25, 65, 68
bedtime restriction 34–35
bedtime routines ix, 9–14, 18–19, 38–40, 68
  on holiday 88–89, 181
bedtime stories 28
biological clock 2
blackout blinds 18, 59, 89, 121
bladder control 86–87
bottle feeding 49–53
boundaries 11–12, 38–39
Bourgeois, Paulette 28
brain development 4
breastfeeding 47–48, 53–58
bruxism (teeth grinding) 134

calmness 26, 66, 92, 111, 178
cerebral palsy (CP) 128–129
children's needs
  loving boundaries 11–12, 38–39
  positive sleep associations 14–16
  right timing 12–14
  safe and pleasant sleep environment 16–19
chronotypes 59–60
circadian clock 2, 6, 37, 129, 130
circadian rhythm 2, 60, 77, 120
clocks 37, 61, 62
Closing the Door 167–169

comforters 14–15, 28, 80
common physical sleep
  problems
  rocking and banging 133–134
  snoring 132–133
  teeth grinding 134
confidence 34, 63, 113, 119,
  152, 178
confusional arousals 68, 70–71
consistency 9, 69, 75, 78, 101,
  111, 178
Controlled Crying 160–161
cortisol 6, 7, 14, 59, 75
co-sleeping 34, 100–101
cots 17, 82–85
CP (cerebral palsy) 128–129
crying
  Controlled Crying 160–161
  and illness 137–138
  new baby 103
  in the night 45, 46, 55, 64,
    67, 70, 114, 154
  stumbling blocks 179–181
  and vomiting 179
cytokines 135

day care and naps
  length of naps 79–80
  timing 78–79
  without you 80
daytime naps 56, 63–64
decision-making 11–12
deep sleep (NREM sleep) 3, 4, 5,
  67, 70, 71, 73
deep sleep problems
  confusional arousals 68,
    70–71

night terrors (sleep terrors)
  60, 67–70, 73
delta sleep 3
dermatitis 139–140
Down's syndrome 130–132,
  133
'dream sleep' (REM sleep) 3, 4,
  5, 64, 73, 75
dreaming 4, 29, 64–67, 73
dummies 14
  case study 95–97
  in day care 80
  saying goodbye to 83, 93–95
duvets 17, 18

early waking 58–60
  and daytime naps 63–64
eczema 139–140
emotional processing 75
explaining to your child 158

falling asleep
  bedtime fears and anxiety
    25–35, 65
  case studies 22
  not wanting to fall asleep
    alone 20–22
  sleep plan 23–24
  taking a long time 35–41
  tips to help your child 36–37
  without you 80
family life
  adopted children 113–118
  bedtime with more than one
    child 103–105
  bringing up children alone
    109–110

grandparents and others
118–119
new baby 100–103
room sharing 28, 106–108, 109
sleepovers with your ex
111–113
fears and anxiety 25–35, 65, 68
Franklin in the Dark 28

gastrointestinal reflux 68
getting up in the morning
174–175
goals 151–152
'golden moments' 159
Gradual Withdrawal 160–161,
169–172
hybrid technique 172–173
grandparents and others
118–119
Gray, Carol 123

head banging 133–134
high temperature 68
holidays
coming home 91
the journey 89–90
plane journeys 90–91
homeostasis 7
homeostatic sleep pressure 7, 13
hormones 2
see also cortisol; melatonin
hospital admissions 140–141
hypnic/hypnagogic jerks 3
hypothalamus 2

ibuprofen 135
identifying sleep problems
149–151

illnesses
longer-term 137–140
minor 134–136
immune system 3

lamps 61
'larks' 59
light sleep (REM sleep) 3, 4, 5,
64, 73, 75
lighting 18, 84
longer-term illnesses 137
asthma 68, 133, 138–139
eczema 139–140
pain 137–138

mattresses 17
melatonin 5–6, 13, 18, 27, 35,
37, 59, 84
and autism 120, 121, 122
and visual impairment 129,
130
memory consolidation 4
milk
at bedtime 11, 37, 48, 49–50,
82–83
case study 49–52
nutrients 48
minor illnesses 134–136
moral support 178
motivation 152–153
moving house 92–93

nappies at night 85
naps 74–75
in daycare 78–80
daytime naps 56, 63–64
disastrous 4 p.m. nap 75,
77–78

and early waking 63–64
falling asleep without you 80
how/when to drop naps 81
keeping them going 63, 75–77
length of naps in day care 79–80
managing naps 78–81
timing 78–79
National Autistic Society 124
neighbours 155
neuromuscular difficulties 128–129
new baby 100–103
night lights 18, 28, 37, 69
night terrors (sleep terrors) 60, 67–70, 73
night waking 13, 42–43
nightmares 64–67, 73
night-time nappies 85
night-time sleep 2–3
night-time sleep problems 13
  bottle-feeding 49–53
  breastfeeding 47–48, 53–58
  case studies 43–47, 49–52, 54–58
  crying 45, 46, 55, 64, 67, 70, 114, 154
  early waking 58–60, 63–64
  getting ready for change 144–145
  night waking 13, 42–47
  nightmares 64–67, 73
  not resettling 142–144
  problems with deep sleep 67–71
  rituals 43–47
  scheduled awakening 60, 70

sleep training clocks and lamps 61–63
sleepwalking 60, 68, 71–73
waking for feeds 47–58
night-time toilet training 86–87
NREM (non-rapid eye movement) sleep 3, 4, 5, 67, 70, 71, 73
nursery 76, 87–88

obstructive sleep apnoea (OSA) 68, 131, 133
older children 103–105
overtiredness 14, 62, 68
'owls' 59–60

pain 137–138
painkillers 134–135, 136, 137
paracetamol, junior 134, 135
pets 28
pillows 17, 83
pineal gland 6
plane journeys 90–91
poorly children
  longer-term illnesses 137–140
  minor illnesses 134–136
  sleeping 134–135
practicalities 154–157

Quick Step Return 161–162

reflux, gastrointestinal 68
REM (rapid eye movement) sleep 3, 4, 5, 64, 73, 75
repetition 9, 14–16
restless leg syndrome 68
rewards 28, 62, 86, 95, 98, 158, 174–175

rocking 133–134
room sharing 28, 106–108, 109
room temperature 18
routines 9–12, 14, 18–19, 68,
   88–89, 181

safety guards 17, 84
scheduled awakening 60, 70
school 87–88
Scope 132
self-settling techniques 160
   case study 164–167
   Closing the Door 167–169
   Controlled Crying 160–161
   evaluating progress, keeping
      going 182–183
   getting up in the morning
      174–175
   Gradual Withdrawal 160–161,
      169–172
   how long will it take 181–182
   hybrid technique 172–173
   making a plan 175–177
   making it work 178
   plan not working? 183–187
   Quick Step Return 161–162
   Standing Quietly 32, 84,
      163–167
   stumbling blocks 178–181
   ten sleep tips 187
   waking in the night 173
   your own sleep needs
      187–190
separation anxiety 20, 25, 65,
   68
serotonin 37
siblings 16, 28, 92, 105, 106,
   154–155

sleep
   circadian rhythm 2, 60, 77,
      120
   delta sleep 3
   how much? 7–8
   need for 1
   at night 2–3
   ten tips 187
   your own needs 187–190
sleep associations 14–16
Sleep Charity, The 132
sleep cues 14–16
sleep cycles 4–5, 5, 21
sleep deprivation 188
sleep diaries 148–149
sleep environment 16
   ambience 18–19
   bed or cot 17, 82
   lighting 18, 84
   room temperature 18
sleep hormones 2, 5–6, 19
   cortisol 6, 7, 14, 59, 75
   melatonin 5–6, 13, 18, 27, 35,
      37, 59, 84, 121, 122, 129,
      130
sleep plan 23–24
   how long will it take? 181
   making a plan and sticking
      with it 175–177
   making it work 178
   stumbling blocks 178–181
sleep practitioners 132
sleep pressure 7, 13, 29–30, 35
sleep problems, identifying
      149–151
sleep restriction 34–35
sleep talking 68
sleep terrors 60, 67–70, 73

sleep training clocks and lamps 61–63
sleep triggers 14–16
sleeping alone 145–147
sleepovers 69, 72
   with your ex 111–113
sleepwalking 60, 68, 71–73
slow wave sleep 3
snoring 132–133
Social Stories™ 123–124
solutions viii–ix
stair gates 72
Standing Quietly 32, 84, 163–167
struggling with sleep 142
   getting ready for change 144–145
   not resettling 142–144
   parents' views 146–147
   reassurance 145–146
stumbling blocks 178–181
support 109

tantrums 40
teeth grinding (bruxism) 134
thoughts and feelings 29
thumb sucking 14, 94, 97–99

time cues (zeitgebers) 130
timing 12–14
toddlers viii
toilet-training, night-time 86–87
transitional objects 14–15, 28
tryptophan 37, 121
TV 10, 19, 37

urine 85, 105, 166

vasopressin 85
visual impairment 129–130
vomiting when crying 179

waking for night-time feeds 47–49
   case studies 49–52, 54–58
waking in the morning 38, 70
waking in the night 66–67, 173
wetting the bed 86–87
white noise 15, 18, 83

'you and me' time 39

zeitgebers (time cues) 130